D0904139

DICTIONARY OF **SHARKS**

$1 95

A Dictionary Of
SHARKS

28

First Edition

Patricia E. Pope

GREAT OUTDOORS PUBLISHING CO.
4747 TWENTY-EIGHTH ST. NORTH
ST. PETERSBURG, FLORIDA 33714

First Edition Published 1973

Pope, Patricia E.   1949 -

A Dictionary of Sharks.

1. Sharks—Identification.   2. Shark Fishing.

I. Title.   II. Title: Sharks.

QL638.9.P63   597′.31   73-7913

ISBN 0-8200-0115-5

PICTURE CREDITS

Galeus piperatus—L.A. County Museum Contributions in Science, no. 10; *Iago omanensis*—Fishery Bulletin, vol. 69; *Halaelurus* spp.—South African Association for Marine Biological Research: Oceanographic Institute, Investigational Report 29; *Halaelurus dawsoni*—Records of the Dominion Museum, vol 7. no. 18; *Hexanchus vitulus* and *H. griseus*—Bulletin of Marine Science, vol. 19 no. 1; *Scyliorhinus retifer*—Proceedings of the Biological Society of Washington, vol. 83, *Triakis fehmanni*—Proceedings of the Biological Society of Washington, vol. 81.

Alopias vulpinus, Carcharhinus limbatus, Carcharodon carcharias, Cephaloscyllium ventrosum, Centroscymnus coleolepsis, Galeus glaucus, Ginglyostoma cirratum, Isurus paucus, Odontaspi tarus, Paramaturus xanurius, Scoliodon terra novae, Somniosus microcephalus, Somniosus pacificus, Sphryna zygaena, Squalus acanthias, Triakis henlei—The Plagiostoma, Garmon, 1913.

ACKNOWLEDGEMENTS

The author would like to express appreciation to Dr. David Baldridge, Dr. Stewart Springer and Mr. Bob Hughes for their assistance.

Contents

Key To Sharks On Cover

1. Whitetip *Carcharhinus longimanus*
2. Bull Shark *Carcharhinus leucas*
3. Tiger *Galeocerdo cuvieri*
4. Porbeagle *Lamna nasus*
5. Basking Shark *Cetorhinus maximus*
6. Sand Shark *Squalus acanthias*
7. Mako *Isurus oxyrinchus*
8. Schroeder's Saw Shark *Pristiophorus schroederi*
9. Brown Shark *Eulamia milberti*

10. Great White *Carcharodon carcharias*
11. Colclough's Shark *Heteroscyllium colcloughi*
12. Great Hammerhead *Sphyrna mokkaran*
13. Nurse Shark *Gingylostoma cirratum*
14. Silvertip *Carcharhinus albimarginatus*
15. Common Thresher *Alopias vulpinus*
16. Frilled Shark *Chlamydoselachus anguineus*

17. Pilot Fish *Naucrates nuctor*
18. Remora *Remora remora*

Twenty-five years ago, Rube Allyn began publishing the Dictionary of Fishes. The Dictionary was designed primarily to help fishermen identify the fish he might catch. But the Dictionary of Fishes could only briefly describe a few of the shark species. Hence, the Dictionary of Sharks— the first lay identification to the sharks of the world. Like its source, the main purpose of this book is to answer that age-old question, "What kind of shark is this?" Shark identification can be difficult, and may hinge on such obscure details as skin folds around the mouth, or teeth number. The sharks described in this book are relatively easy to identify, and each entry is pictured. Entries are arranged in alphabetical order by genera.

The sharks we know today evolved from jawless lamprey-like fishes about 400 million years ago. This was during the heyday of the crinoids— those flower-like relatives of the sea urchins, and during the very beginnings of the armoured fishes.

Detailed knowledge of the earliest shark was non-existant until the late 1880's, when an amateur archeologist found fossil shark remains in an ancient mud bed south of Cleveland, Ohio. This shark was called *Cladoselache*, meaning "branch-ed-toothed shark". Like many of today's sharks, *Cladoselache* had a rough skin, a keel on each side of the tail base, and a clearly defined lateral line.

Both dorsal fins were small, and the mouth was filled with diminuative, pointed teeth. With a few changes in body silouette and tooth conformation, *Cladoselache* is practically indistinguishable from modern sharks.

Evolution was pretty rapid; by the Mississipian Era, 320 million years ago, shell-crushing sharks like the Port Jackson Shark had appeared. Since this modern-day shark feeds on shellfish, the diet of its ancestor may well have contributed to the downfall of the trilobites, small relatives of the horseshoe crab. Another one of the fossil sharks was an ancestor of the Great White Shark. Fossil teeth from this behemouth can measure six inches in length. A little extrapolation gives us a 60-foot shark that must have required considerable food. This particular species died out though, and by the end of the upper Paleozoic (about 280 million years ago), many kinds of sharks had appeared and distribution was world-wide.

Presently the sharks of the world are separated into 19 families. This number may change, however, as we learn more about sharks. Two or more families may be grouped together under a new family name. Often groupings as large as families are split into two or more families as more members are discovered. The largest family is the Carcharhinidae, with over 60 member species. As you might suspect, this largest family also has the greatest number of species known to

Shark Families

Alopiidae: Thresher Sharks
Carcharhiniade: Requiem Sharks
Cetorhinidae: Basking Shark
Chlamydoselache: Frilled Shark
Heterodontidae: Bullhead Sharks
Hexanchidae: Six- and Seven-Gilled Sharks
Isuridae: Mackerel Sharks
Odontaspidae: Sand Sharks
Orectolobidae: Nurse and Carpet Sharks
Oxynotidae: Spine-Finned Sharks
Pristiophoridae: Saw Sharks
Pseudotriakidae: False Cat Sharks
Rhincodontidae: Whale Sharks
Scapanorhynchidae: Goblin Sharks
Scyliorhinidae: Cat Sharks
Sphyrnidae: Hammerhead Sharks
Squalidae: Spiny Dogfish
Squatinidae: Angel Sharks'
Triakidae: Smooth Dogfish

attack man. On the other extreme, several families have only a single member each.

Looking at sharks as a whole, it is pretty easy to pick out at least some of the characteristics used to identify them. Basically, a shark is a shark because he possesses seven characteristics: a streamlined shape, five to seven paired gill openings, sandpaper-like scales, and a cartilagenous body with jaws, teeth, and paired fins. These points separate the sharks from the true bony fish, rays, porpoises and lampreys.

If you look more closely, the differences between sharks and other sea creatures become more pronounced. For instance, shark teeth are arranged to assure a full set of chompers at any given time—even if several teeth broke off last week. This is accomplished by having several complete sets of teeth in the mouth at a time. The functional set—the set currently in use—is fully erupted and sits on the edge of the jaw. The back-up sets are just behind this first set, with the set closest to the functional set the most erect. The other sets are covered with mouth tissue, the amount of covering depending on the distance from the functional set. The further away the tooth set, the more is hidden by tissue. If one or more teeth are lost from the functional set, the corresponding tooth from the next row moves forward into place. Interestingly enough, all these teeth are attached to a fibous layer on the surface of the jaw bone. Opening the mouth pulls this fibrous tissue forward, which in turn brings the teeth forward and pointing out. This tooth movement enables the shark to bite firmly and to hang on to what he bites.

A close look at the inner edge of a shark's jaw. The upper teeth are the erect set. The other sets lie flat against each other and the jawbone.

Unlike the bony fish, sharks have no swim bladder. This makes them heavier than water and they must swim constantly, both to keep from sinking, and to provide a constant stream of oxygenated water to the gills. But there is a way around this requirement. Some sharks have a spiracle (a hole through which water can deliver oxygen directly to the gills) behind each eye

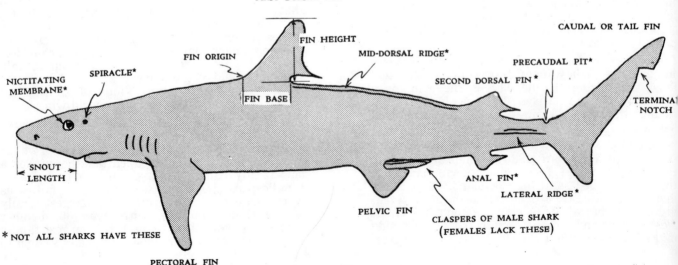

FIRST DORSAL FIN

FIN HEIGHT

CAUDAL OR TAIL FIN

FIN ORIGIN

MID-DORSAL RIDGE*

PRECAUDAL PIT*

SECOND DORSAL FIN *

NICTITATING MEMBRANE*

SPIRACLE*

FIN BASE

TERMINAL NOTCH

SNOUT LENGTH

ANAL FIN*

LATERAL RIDGE*

PELVIC FIN

CLASPERS OF MALE SHARK (FEMALES LACK THESE)

* NOT ALL SHARKS HAVE THESE

PECTORAL FIN

Sharks possessing spiracles can rest on the bottom and wait for dinner to happen along instead of actively hunting. The Carpet Sharks are a good example of this. Correspondingly, their appearance has modified to permit them to blend in with the bottom. Sometimes they blend in so well they get stepped on.

Compared with the sedentary life of the Carpet Sharks, other sharks are true vagabonds. Some swim as far as 35,000 miles yearly in breeding and migratory patterns. As they wander, their color may change. A shark that ventures from deep to shallow water will change color from deep grey or black to a pale brown or grey. For example, the Bull Shark is normally a dark or light grey with a white stomach. Yet when these sharks venture into fresh water—as they often do—the underside becomes a pale brown, more in keeping with the muddy waters of the lakes and rivers they must traverse. As yet, we don't know what drives Bull Sharks to wend their way upstream to a freshwater lake. Not all of them make it; some seem to go only part-way up and then return to the ocean. Others go all the way up the stream and spend the rest of their lives in the lake. In any case, the sharks must make the journey by themselves; the Pilotfish and Remoras that might ordinarily accompany them cannot take the change from salt to freshwater. Either these companions leave the shark, or they die. It seems doubtful that this shark "migration" is reproduction-motivated, as it is in salmon. Bull Shark young are normally estuarine-born.

Sharks reproduce by one of three ways. The first and most primitive way is by simple egg-laying. Both the horn and catshark families reproduce this way. Shape of the egg case may vary, from rectangular to conical, but most have tendrils issuing from one or more corners to serve as anchors. Laid in pairs, the eggs hatch in six to ten months.

The majority of sharks merely retain the eggs until they hatch. Among this group are the Thresher Sharks, the Sand Sharks, and the Makos. This egg-retention is carried one step further for the Smooth Dogfish, the Blue Shark, and for some members of the family Carcharhinidae. After the yolk is consumed and the egg hatches within the female, a placental-like attachment forms and the young sharks are nourished from the female's body, much the same way mammalian embryos are nourished before birth.

As a whole, shark young are born on nursery grounds for that particular species of shark, after a gestation period of about one year. Near the end of this gestation, the females travel to the nursery grounds. Once on the grounds, the gravid females stop feeding completely. This is to the very real advantage of the baby sharks; a hungry female could decimate the young shark population in a short time. Males do not come onto the nusery grounds, and they continue to feed normally offshore. Previously, during the breeding season, the males did not feed. At that time, courtship was anything but courtly. If the female was big and cranky enough, the male may have had trouble in avoiding death, much less in mating. Couple this with the fact that the male's strength was down because he hadn't been eating, and you'll understand why fewer males ended the breeding season than began it.

Egg case of the Filetail Catshark, (Paramaturus xaniurus).

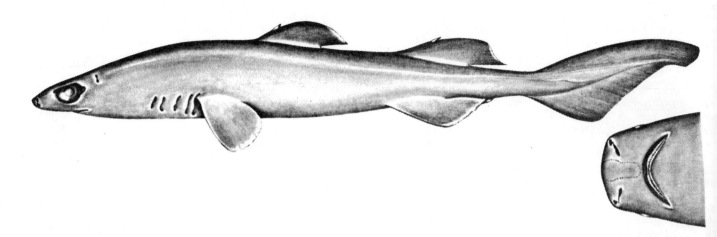

● BLACK SHARK   *Acueloa nigera*

A deep-water shark, the Black Shark has been found only off the coasts of Chili and Peru. The flaccid, soft body is better able to withstand the crushing pressures of the great depths it inhabits than the tough, less elastic skin of other sharks.

Identifying Characteristics: Large eyes; tips of fins white, the amount being greater in younger specimens; upper lobe of tail with terminal notch. Snout almost bluntly squared off.

Size: Females grow to almost 2 ft.; males a little smaller.

Color: Body uniformly black, with white-tipped fins.

Range: Deep water off Peru and Chili.

● BIGEYE THRESHER SHARK
Alopias superciliosus

The elongated tail of the Bigeye Thresher is used to round up the small fishes it feeds on. Swimming in a tight circle around schooling fish, the shark groups them into a close bunch, and begins feeding. A shark of the deep seas, the Bigeye Thresher can be distinguished from the other thresher sharks by its large eyes, longer snout, and fewer teeth in the jaws.

Identifying Characteristics: Big eyes; prominent crest on top of head; pelvic and first dorsal fins almost same size; longer snout than Common Thresher; tip of first dorsal overlaps origin of pelvic fins.

Size: 18 ft.

Color: Dark brown/grey above, with some iridescence.

Range: Warm and tropical waters of all oceans, rather rare.

Brown Cat Shark

COMMON THRESHER *Alopias vulpinus*

Threshers are also guilty of creating some controversy in the scientific world. Some sources claim there are four species; others insist that only two species can be recognized. Whatever the result of the controversy, the Common Thresher is well enough known and recognized to be safe from the confusion.

Identifying Characteristics: Long tail, used when circling groups of small fishes to scare the fishes into a group that can be fed from easily. Small eyes.

Size: Grows to a little more than 19 ft. and 1000 lbs.

Color: Upper surfaces shades of dark brown or grey to black. Lower surface pale, but underside of snout may be as dark as upper surface.

Range: Warm and subtropical waters of both oceans.

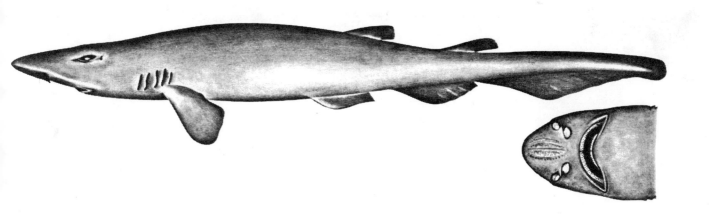

BROWN CAT SHARK *Apisturus brunneus*

This elongated shark from the eastern coast of the Pacific is characterized by the shovel-shaped nose and small pectoral fins.

Identifying Characteristics: Dorsal fins close together and set far back on body; eyes narrow and long; head flattened and pointed.

Size: Usually between 1 ft. 10 inches, and 2 ft. 2 in.

Color: Body warm brown on both upper and lower surfaces.

Range: Eastern Pacific from British Columbia to Baja California.

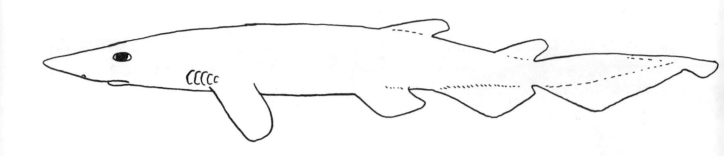

● DEEP-WATER CAT SHARK

Apisturus profundorum

The gill-rakers protruding from the gill openings serve to separate this shark from other members of the catshark family.

Identifying Characteristics: Gill rakers protruding from gill openings; caudal fin nearly 1/3 total body length; second dorsal fin originates above middle of anal fin (fins terminate opposite each other); large anal fin.

Size: Probably less than 2 ft.

Color: Grey-brown on both sides of body.

Range: Known only from the Continental Shelf off Delaware Bay.

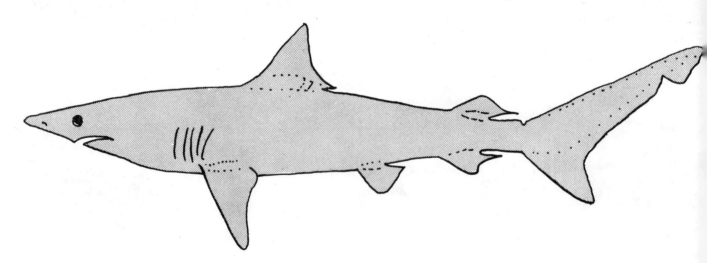

● FINETOOTH SHARK *Aprionodon isodon*

Both jaws of the Finetooth are filled with straight, smooth-edged teeth. This apparently rare inshore species feeds on the variety of small fishes it finds there.

Identifying Characteristics: Smooth-edged, straight teeth, similar in both jaws. Well-developed furrows around the mouth. Second dorsal fin orginates over the anal fin (this point helps distinguish it from Sharpnose Shark whose second dorsal originates behind the anal fin).

Size: Usually about 4 ft.

Color: Bluish-grey above, grey sides, and white below.

Range: Rare; coastal areas of the tropical Atlantic, north to New York.

● SPOTTED DOGFISH   *Assymbolus analis*

One of the many catsharks with spots, the Spotted Dogfish can be distinguished by its long anal fin base. The base of the anal fin can be as much as twice the length of the base of either of the dorsal fins.

Identifying Characteristics: Fold in skin below lower jaw extending for ⅓ the distance to the jaw hinge. Long anal fin base; ventral fins of males connected by a membrane behind the claspers.

Size: More than 2 ft.

Color: Light brown with rusty spots, usually half the size of the eye.

Range: Australia, from New South Wales to Victoria; Tasmania; south and southwestern Australia. May occur as deep as 200 ft.

● MARBLED CATSHARK
Atelomycterus macleyi

Flaps of skin from the edges of the nostrils lie over the edge of the upper lip in this shark. Tastefully patterned in a quiet series of spots, the Marbled Catshark is often mistakenly identified as other catshark species.

Identifying Characteristics: Nasal flap lying just over the edge of upper lip; small spiracle near eye; eye rounded and small; egg case has tendrils at one end only.

Size: 2 ft.

Color: Shades of brown-grey with darker brown spots. Spots often arranged in bands around body.

Range: North Australia, and perhaps northwestern Australia and Queensland.

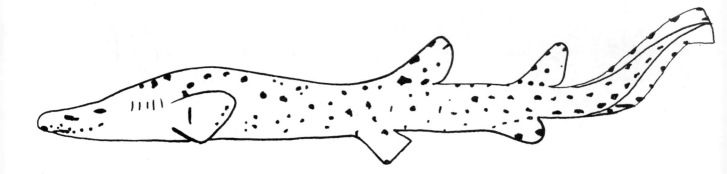

● **BLACK-SPOTTED CATSHARK**
Aulohalalurus labiosus

The catshark family is quite distinct in lacking nictating membrance, the "third eyelid" that travels from the inner corner of the eye to the outer corner. The Black-spotted Catshark has very long labial fold that almost surrounds the mouth.

Identifying Characteristics: Nostrils close together; teeth in lower jaw larger than in upper; head much depressed; elongate body, with vent before middle of body.

Size: Slightly more than 2 ft.

Color: Brown above, lighter below. Upper surface with black dots.

Range: Southwestern Australia.

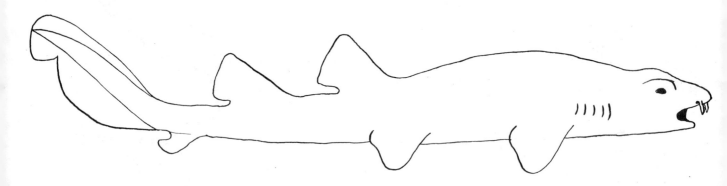

● **BLIND SHARK** *Brachaleurus waddi*

Usually found among rocks and rocky fore-shores, the Blind Shark is most easily identified by the long barbel dangling from the edge of each nostril. It breeds in November, the beginning of summer in Australia. Perhaps as an adaptation to the shallow waters it inhabits, this shark can live a long time out of water.

Identifying Characteristics: Head flattened; single barbel dangling from each nostril; deep groove just below lower jaw; spiracle below eye; first dorsal fin behind pelvics.

Size: 3 ft.

Color: Dark coffee-brown to blackish. Young specimens may have additional small white dots and flecks, with darker brown vertical bands.

Range: Australia, both in the New South Wales and southern Queensland areas.

● SILVERTIP SHARK

Carcharhinus albimarginatus

The pointed white tip of this shark's first dorsal fin is the most salient identification point. The pointed pectoral and dorsal fins serve to distinguish it from both the Reef and Oceanic Whitetip Sharks. Like the Galapagos Shark, the Silvertip damages tuna nets and eats the netted tuna.

Identifying Characteristics: Snout rounded; pectorals long and slender; first dorsal with a free tip; teeth notched in upper jaw.

Size: Average about 8 ft.

Color: Light grey.

Range: Temperate coastal Pacific waters. Larger specimens may venture into deeper water.

● BIGNOSE SHARK   *Carcharhinus altimus*

Often a distinct coppery-red color, this shark seems to prefer deep waters. It is rarely caught in waters less than 400 ft. deep. Night may find it in shallow waters.

Identifying Characteristics: Nostrils have an obvious finger-like lobe; very prominent dorsal ridge; snout moderately pointed.

Size: Maximum size about 9 ft.; 25 in. at birth.

Color: Greyish-brown above, sides a lighter tint. Also occurs a coppery-red color, but this shade fades to grey after death. Dirty white below.

Range: Tropical Pacific; West Indian area.

Silky Shark

● **SILKY SHARK**   *Carcharhinus falciformis*

If it is possible for a shark to be considered "smooth-skinned", the Silky deserves this title. Its scales are small and compressed; this gives the skin a relatively smooth texture. The Silky enjoys the dubious distinction of being the most abundant and the most destructive shark to the tuna industry in the tropical Pacific.

Identifying Characteristics: Besides the smooth skin, the Silky is characterized by a mid-dorsal ridge, a moderately pointed snout, and unsymmetrical upper teeth that are notched on one side. First dorsal fin is not as high as in the Sandbar Shark. Pectoral fins long and slender.

Size: Maximum size 10 ft. The largest reported to Great Outdoors weighed 500 lbs., but no length was recorded. Richard Thorton of Durham, N.C., caught the shark at Nags Head, N.C.

Color: Grey to black above, shading to white below.

Range: Common in tropical belt of western Atlantic and Pacific. Waters of outer continental shelf, and also in the deep sea where the waters are warm.

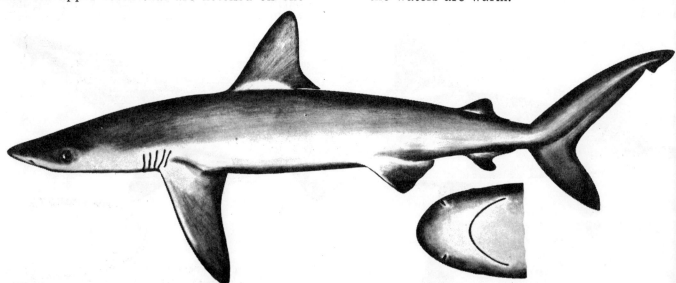

● **GALAPAGOS SHARK**
           Carcharhinus galapagensis

Tuna fishermen hate to see the high, erect first dorsal fin of this aggressive shark coming towards their nets; this is one of the sharks that habitually damages tuna nets and devours netted tuna. It is verified as an attacker in the Atlantic.

Identifying Characteristics: Front margin of first dorsal nearly straight. Pectorals taper to a sharp tip; snout broadly rounded; mid-dorsal ridge present. Second dorsal relatively high with rear margin deeply concave.

Size: 12 ft.

Color: Grey-brown.

Range: Offshore islands in the eastern tropical Pacific. One report of occurrence in the Atlantic.

14

Blacktip Shark

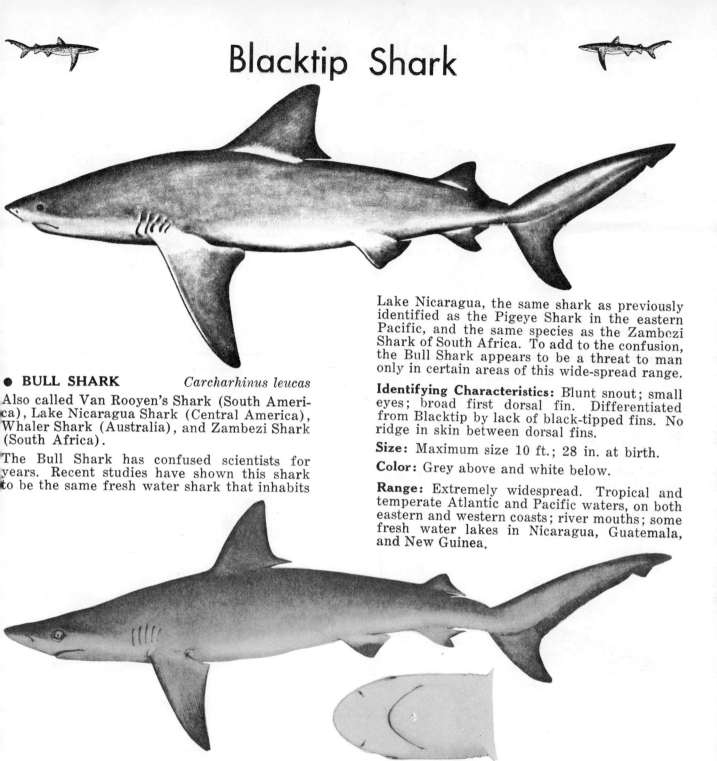

● BULL SHARK *Carcharhinus leucas*

Also called Van Rooyen's Shark (South America), Lake Nicaragua Shark (Central America), Whaler Shark (Australia), and Zambezi Shark (South Africa).

The Bull Shark has confused scientists for years. Recent studies have shown this shark to be the same fresh water shark that inhabits Lake Nicaragua, the same shark as previously identified as the Pigeye Shark in the eastern Pacific, and the same species as the Zambezi Shark of South Africa. To add to the confusion, the Bull Shark appears to be a threat to man only in certain areas of this wide-spread range.

Identifying Characteristics: Blunt snout; small eyes; broad first dorsal fin. Differentiated from Blacktip by lack of black-tipped fins. No ridge in skin between dorsal fins.

Size: Maximum size 10 ft.; 28 in. at birth.

Color: Grey above and white below.

Range: Extremely widespread. Tropical and temperate Atlantic and Pacific waters, on both eastern and western coasts; river mouths; some fresh water lakes in Nicaragua, Guatemala, and New Guinea.

● BLACKTIP SHARK *Carcharhinus limbatus*

The Blacktip and Spinner sharks are very closely related. Because of this, they present a confusing problem. They have been shuffled through a bewildering series of common names, in an effort to clarify their relationship. It hasn't worked very well. Perhaps the easiest way to distinguish between the two is to examine the lower teeth. The Spinner's teeth will be smooth; the Blacktip's, finely serrated. It is important, however, that both the sharks be dead before an examination is attempted.

Identifying Characteristics: Tip of fins black; lower teeth finely serrated. Eyes larger and gill slits shorter than in the Spinner Shark. Schools; characteristic leaps and rolls make it a prized game fish.

Size: 7 ft. Great Outdoors record 6 ft. 8 in., 158 lbs. Caught by Brian Martel at Boca Grande, Florida, May 5, 1973.

Color: Dark grey, dusky bronze, slate blue above. White or yellow below.

Range: Tropical and subtropical seas of both oceans.

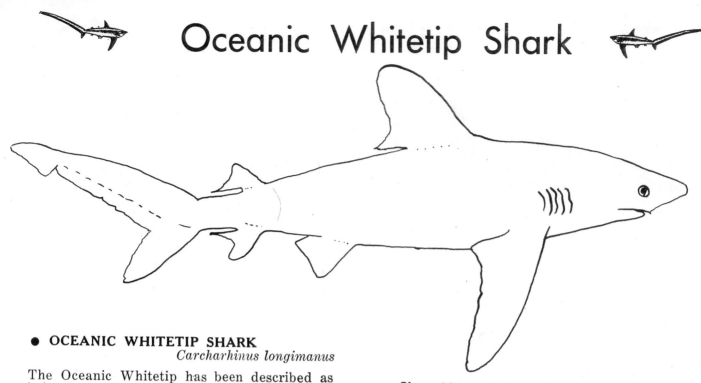

OCEANIC WHITETIP SHARK
Carcharhinus longimanus

The Oceanic Whitetip has been described as being insensitive to pain. Stewart Springer, one of the world's foremost authorities on sharks, has stated that "I do not know of anything except a beaker of formalin poured down the gullet that elicits a very strong reaction." Other than this characteristic, it is most easily recognized by the white-tipped fins.

Identifying Characteristics: Broadly rounded, white-tipped first dorsal fin; short snout. The free rear tip of the anal fin reaches very nearly to the base of the tail.

Size: About 27 in. at birth, growing to a maximum of 12 ft.

Color: Greyish-brown, light grey or pale brown on upper surface. Pale yellow or dirty white below.

Range: Offshore waters in depths of over 600 ft. Warm waters of the Atlantic, Gulf of Mexico, Caribbean and Pacific.

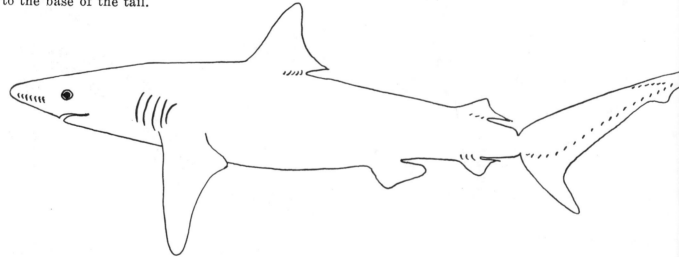

SPINNER SHARK
Carcharhinus maculipinnis

Known to attack humans, this good-sized shark has smaller eyes than the Blacktip Shark. Its range is more restricted than the Blacktip, and isn't considered as good a game fish.

Identifying Characteristics: Smooth lower teeth; small eyes; long gill slits; no dorsal ridge. Black-tipped fins.

Size: 8 ft. The largest on record at Great Outdoors was caught by Kathryn Herwitt of Monroeville, Pa., off Abaco, Bahamas. Her Spinner weighed 305 lbs. and measured 7 ft.

Color: Much the same as the Blacktip, varying from bronze to dull blue to grey with a white belly.

Range: Tropical and subtropical Atlantic.

Dusky Shark

SANDBAR SHARK *Carcharhinus milberti*

Birth defects are found in all animals, yet it may come as some surprise to you to learn the Sandbar Shark is no exception. For every 500 to 1000 litters of Sandbar pups, one litter will be born mouthless. Besides lacking mouths, the eyes will be set close together, and on the *underside* of the snout.

Identifying Characteristics: Large first dorsal fin (vertical height more than 10% of shark's total length). Second dorsal orginates directly opposite anal fin. Free tip of second dorsal as long as base. First dorsal originates in advance of pectoral axilla.

Size: Averages 6½ ft. Maximum 7 ft. 8 in.

Color: Ranges from grey to brown above, paler below. Definite bronze tinge.

Range: Chiefly an Atlantic shark, from the Caribbean to Cape Cod. May also be found in the Mediterranean and areas of the eastern Atlantic.

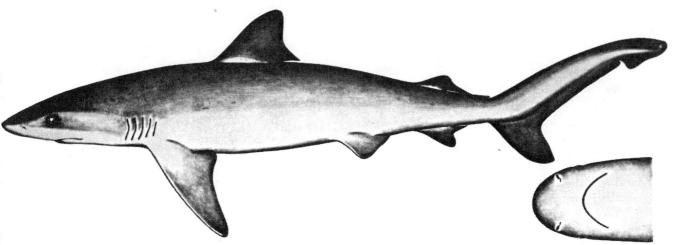

DUSKY SHARK *Carcharhinus obscurus*

This is one of the few sharks known to migrate in sexually segregated groups. The eastern Atlantic population migrates yearly from Florida to New Jersey, where the young are born.

Identifying Characteristics: Second dorsal fin 1½ times longer than high; distinct dorsal ridge between fins. Pectoral fins shorter and eye larger than found in Silky Shark.

Size: Averages about 9 ft., but may occasionally grow to 11 ft. The largest on record at Great Outdoors weighed 825 lbs. It was taken at Blind Pass, St. Petersburg Beach, Fla., by Bob Hughes.

Color: Blue, copper or grey above, white below.

Range: Found in both Pacific and Atlantic waters, in tropical and temperate regions.

17

Smalltail Shark

● **SMALLTAIL SHARK**

Carcharhinus porosus

The most distinctive thing about this rather small shark is the first dorsal fin. The rear margin of the dorsal is often ragged, much like the edge of a flag that has blown in the breeze for too long. Other sharks may have torn first dorsal fins, but this is the only species with such pronounced tattering.

Identifying Characteristics: Upper and lower precaudal pits distinct; lower teeth only finely serrated. Second dorsal originates well behind the origin of the anal fin.

Size: Commonly about 3 ft.; may grow to 4 ft.

Color: Medium grey or brown.

Range: Coastal waters of the temperate and tropical Pacific; western Atlantic.

● **NARROWTOOTH SHARK**

Carcharhinus remotus

The Narrowtooth Shark starts out life as a fairly slim shark. But, like most of us, it puts on weight as it matures, and reaches adulthood as a stocky shark. The lower teeth of this heavyset fish are serrated, but the cusps are so small it is hard to see them without magnification.

Identifying Characteristics: Cusps of upper teeth larger than cusps of lower teeth; nostrils with short lobe; origin of second dorsal sometimes behind origin of anal fin.

Size: 9 ft. maximum length.

Color: Usually dark shades of grey, occasionally brown.

Range: Western Atlantic and Eastern Pacific chiefly in southern hemisphere. Rarely in northern hemisphere.

18

● REEF SHARK   *Carcharhinus springeri*

The Reef Shark is a relative newcomer to the world of known sharks. Although it was not described until 1944, it appears to be a common shark in the inshore water of its range. It can be distinguished from its close relative, the Dusky Shark, by its more angular and erect first dorsal fin.

Identifying Characteristics: Dorsal ridge present; eyes relatively large. Distance between pelvic and anal fins less than ¾ length of anal fin base. Length of second dorsal greater than height.

Size: Grows from a birth length of 38 in., to an adult length of 8 ft.

Color: Olive-grey above; paler shades of grey-yellow below.

Range: Inshore reefs, less frequently open waters of the Bahama banks; West Indies; and the S.E. Florida coast.

● PICO BLANCO   *Carcharhinus velox*

A black spot on the snout, surrounded by white, identifies this shark of the tropical Pacific. The snout itself is extremely elongated.

Identifying Characteristics: Nostrils located almost on the sides of the snout, and close to each other; teeth of the upper jaw serrated.

Size: Common up to 4 ft. in length; occasionally found measuring up to 5 ft.

Color: Brown-grey.

Range: Coastal waters of the temperate and tropical eastern Pacific.

GREAT WHITE SHARK
Carcharodon carcharias

This is the shark people think of first when they hear the cry "Shark!". Known to be a maneater, this widespread shark also goes by the chilling name of White Death. Ironically enough, it often ends up on the dinnertable labled "swordfish".

Identifying Characteristics: Crescent-shaped tail; large, triangular serrated teeth. Anal fin originates behind origin of second dorsal fin.

Size: Lengths of 15 ft. not uncommon. The record specimen reportedly measured 36½ ft. but the identification may have been in error. Largest authenticated was 16 ft. 10 in. Caught at Ceduna, S. Australia, by Alfred Dean.

Color: Leaden grey, dull grey-blue, gray-brown or dark grey above, shading to white below. Often has a dark spot at the base of the pectoral fin.

Range: World-wide; temperate, sub-tropical and tropical waters of both Atlantic and Pacific Oceans.

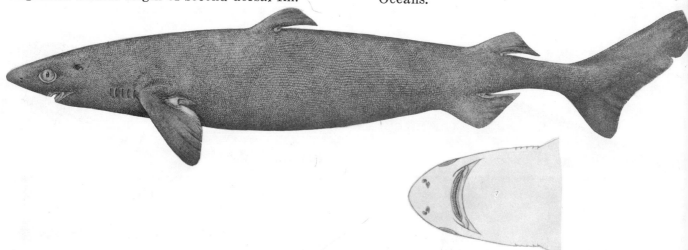

PORTUGESE SHARK
Centroscymnus coelolepsis

The habits of this deep-water shark are not very well known. It has been reported in waters ranging from 840 feet, to a record depth of 8917 ft.

Identifying Characteristics: Lacks anal fin. Dorsal spines in front of each dorsal fin; tail blunted and rounded at tip; large eyes; small dorsal fin.

Size: Largest caught measured 3 ft. 8 in. Nine inches at birth.

Color: Dark brown.

Range: Both sides of the Northern Atlantic. Range southward not established.

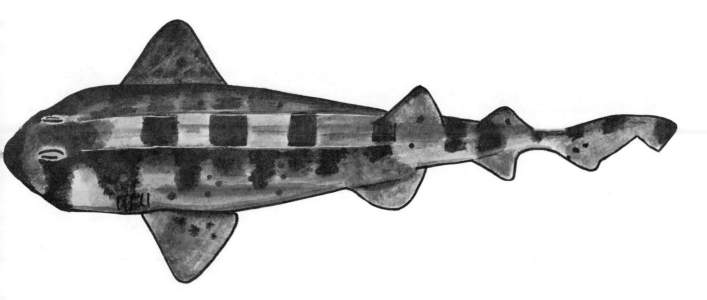

● DRAUGHTSBOARD SHARK
Cephaloscyllium isabella

When captured, this sleepy-looking shark is said to give a barking sound, much like that of a dog. The sleepy appearance is due to its slit-like eyes; the shark prefers deep water and seems to shun more open space. Despite its large size (8 ft.), it is considered harmless; it feeds on crustaceans and sea worms.

Identifying Characteristics: Checkered pattern; body can be expanded, much like a blowfish; head oval in cross-section; body tear-drop shaped, with greatest width between pectoral fins; anal fin base length equal to distance between anal fin and caudal fin.

Size: To 8 ft.

Color: Grey-brown with poorly-defined checkerboard on back.

Range: New Zealand.

● SWELL SHARK
Cephaloscyllium ventriosum

Like the Blowfish, the Swell Shark puffs up with air when caught. This is probably a defense mechanism, serving to convince most of the Swell Shark predators that he's too big to eat.

Identifying Characteristics: Body robust; head broad, with short, blunt snout; variegated color pattern; no labial grooves at corners of mouth.

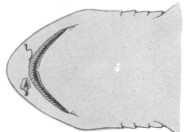

Size: To 3 1/3 ft.

Color: Brown above, with vague saddles and blotches of darker brown; small black spots over entire surface of body. Underside pale.

Range: Eastern Pacific, from California to Chili.

● **HEAD SHARK**   *Cephalurus cephalus*

A small species from deep water, the Head Shark hasn't been collected since 1908; and there is a grand total of two specimens on record. For all that, however, it is rather an interesting shark, seemingly all head.

Identifying Characteristics: Flattened, wide head; large eyes; round, widely spaced gill slits.

Size: 1⅓ ft.

Color: Uniform brown, both on upper and lower surfaces.

Range: Gulf of California and Revillagigedo Islands.

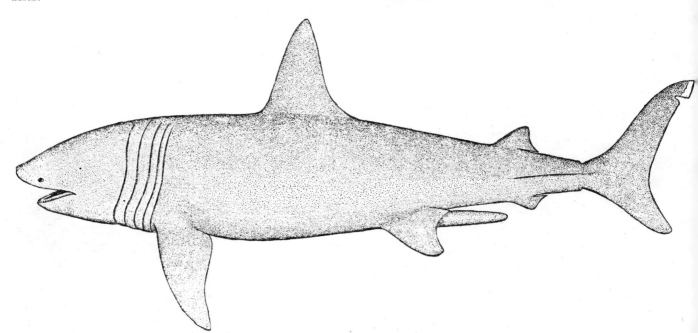

● **BASKING SHARK**   *Cetorhinus maximus*

The Basking Shark is remarkable for several reasons. A filter-feeder of considerable size (possibly more than 32 ft.), it often travels in schools numbering upwards of 100. Evidence now indicates that in winter the Basking Sharks lose their gill rakers, sink to the bottom, and hibernate.

Identifying Characteristics: Tail fin crescent-shaped; enormously long gill slits; numerous tiny teeth; gill rakers; ridge on each side of body near tail.

Size: To 32 ft., and possibly up to 40.

Color: Greyish-black.

Range: Temperate zones on both side of equator.

Frilled Shark

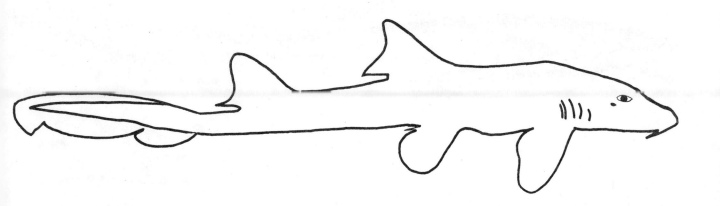

● **BROWN-BANDED CATSHARK**
Chiloscyllium punctatum

The gills of this Australian shark are often infested by a small crustacean. Until the infestation becomes heavy, it appears to have no real effect on the health of the shark.

Identifying Characteristics: Fourth and fifth gill slits close together; snout rounded; scales large and polished in appearance; nasal area deeply grooved.

Size: To slightly less than 3 ft.

Color: Rusty-brown, somewhat darker on sides and tail. Young may be darkly banded.

Range: Northern Australia.

● **FRILLED SHARK**
Chlamydoselachus anguinus

This snake-like shark closely resembles mariners' descriptions of sea serpents. Extremely thin, a five-foot long specimen may have a diameter of only four inches. The first gill slit extends under the chin from one side of the head to the other. All the gill covers are exaggerated, giving the shark the appearance of wearing a Victorian ruff. The only member of its family, the closest relatives we can identify from fossil teeth date from 12 to 20 million years ago.

Identifying Characteristics: Ruffled gill covers, with first gill slit extending under the chin from one side to the other. Long, thin body, with fins located well back.

Size: Largest reported 6 feet 4 inches, more often near 5 feet.

Color: Dark grey.

Range: Deep waters off Japan, Iberian Peninsula, North Africa, Scotland, Norway, Ireland. Distribution may be world-wide, but in waters so deep as to be almost inaccessible.

Slipper Shark

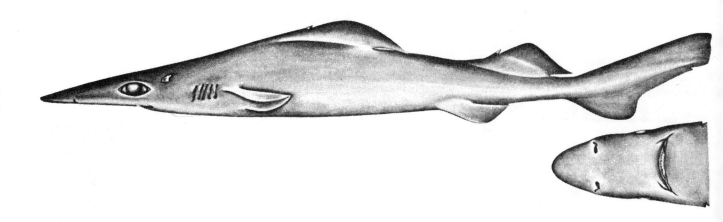

● **SLIPPER SHARK** *Deania calcea*

The snout of the Slipper Shark is extremely long and flattened, much like the toe of a slipper. Its large eyes indicate it is a deep-sea shark.

Identifying Characteristics: Elongated, pointed snout; length of first dorsal fin 3 times greater than height; no anal fin; spines in front of dorsal.

Size: 3 1/3 ft.

Color: Grey.

Range: Waters off central Chili.

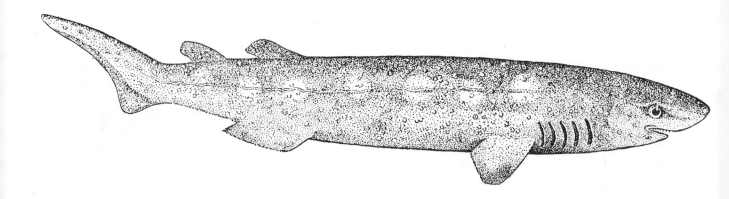

● **COMMON BRAMBLE SHARK**
Echinorhinus brucus

The body and fins of this shark are scattered with large button-like dermal denticles (enlarged scales). Each denticle is topped with one or more curved spines, giving the shark a very rough and rather pebbled appearance. It is warned that rough contact with the skin will cause some pain.

Identifying Characteristics: Button-like denticles, usually a little more than ½ inch across. Each topped with at least one spine.

Size: The record Bramble Shark was caught off Buenas Aires in 1898. It measured 10 ft.

Color: Shades of dark grey-brown.

Range: Tropical to temperate waters, in depths ranging from 60 to 600 ft. More common in eastern Atlantic than western Atlantic. Also found in the Mediterranean, around Japan, Hawaii and New Zealand.

Slime Shark

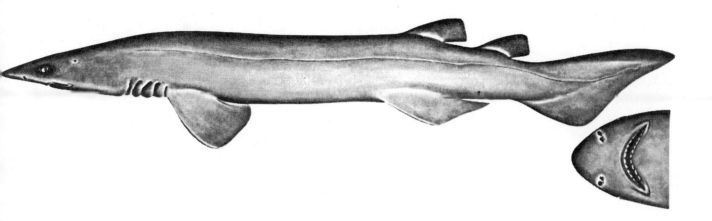

● PRICKLY SHARK *Echinorhinus cookei*

The Prickly Shark can be distinguished from its close relative, the Common Bramble Shark, by its denticle (scale) size. The Bramble Shark has rather large, sparsely spaced scales; a 6½ ft. specimen may have scales more than ½ inch wide. In contrast, the scales of a Prickly Shark of the same size will be only 1/6 inch across.

Identifying Characteristics: First dorsal fin located far back on body; scales spiney and about 1/6 wide. Body does not taper as sharply as other sharks; large pelvic fins.

Size: Rarely larger than 13 ft.

Color: Medium to dark grey.

Range: Appears to be uncommon. Recorded off southern California; Guadaloupe Island, Peru, and the Hawaiian Islands.

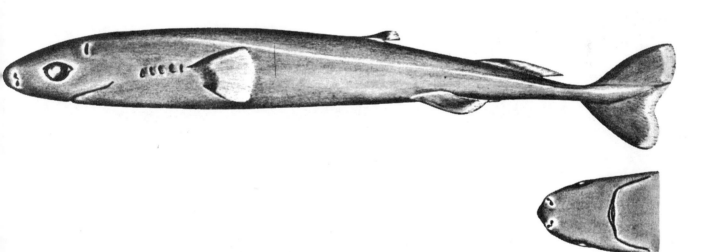

● SLIME SHARK *Euprotomicrus bispinatus*

The elongated, fusiform body of this shark deviates strongly from what one considers to be the usual shark shape. The narrowly blunted snout and almost squared-off mouth also serve to separate the Slime Shark from the other sharks.

Identifying Characteristics: Base of second dorsal more than twice as long as the base of the first dorsal fin; body fusiform; margins of fins uncolored and clear.

Size: Less than 1 ft.

Color: Brown to black.

Range: Midwater Pacific; reported from California and Hawaii.

Arum Shark

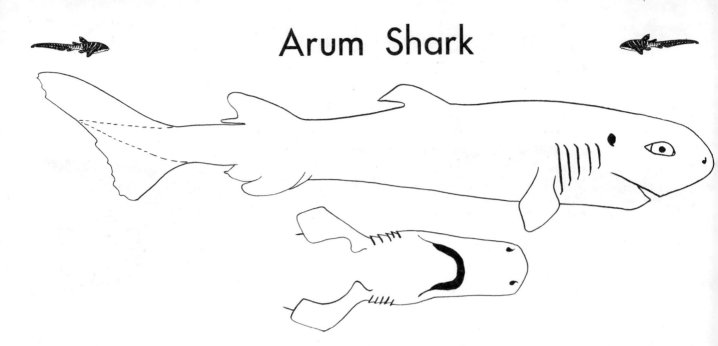

● ARUM SHARK
Euprotomicroides zantedeschia

The single specimen of this small shark was trawled off the west coast of South Africa in 1963. The shark resembles the *Euprotomicrus* sharks (like the Slime Shark) in general shape, but has a heavier body, longer gill slits, and first and second dorsal fins of almost the same size.

Identifying Characteristics: Large gill slits, increasing in size from first to fifth. Second dorsal fin only slightly larger than first dorsal. Second dorsal directly over pelvic fins. Head bulbous, with bluntly rounded snout. Spiracle large.

Size: 7½ inches.

Color: Brown. Lower surfaces of snout, lower lip, belly and claspers black.

Range: Known only from single specimen trawled west of Cape Town, South Africa, between 1500 and 2100 feet of water.

● SAWTAIL SHARK   *Figaro boardmani*

The Sawtail shark is named for the series of enlarged denticles along the top and bottom edges of the tail. In the larger specimens, the back is humped as in the specimen shown. This is apparently one of the sharks that travels in sexually segregated groups, as all the specimens trawled have been males.

Identifying Characteristics: Enlarged denticles along upper and lower edges of tail; large crossbar pattern on back, extending downwards only to lateral line after first dorsal; humpback in larger specimens.

Size: 2 ft.

Color: Light grey background, on which are scattered darker crossbands of brown-grey; these cross bands often interspersed with lighter brown areas; inside of mouth light brownish-grey.

Range: Australia; New South Wales and Bass Strait.

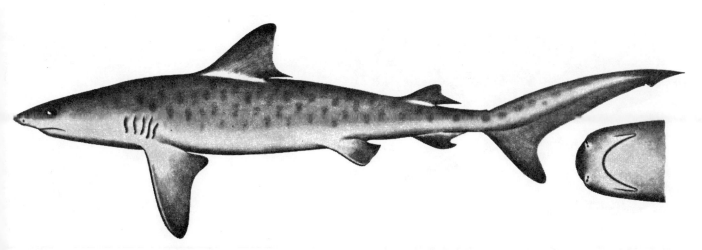

● **TIGER SHARK** *Galeocerdo cuviere*

Younger specimens of this species, up to lengths of 5 or 6 ft., can be identified by the dark, irregular bars on the sides and fins. These "stripes" are what give the Tiger Shark its common name. Its behavior confirms the common name, too — the Tiger Shark is justifiably feared as a maneater.

Identifying Characteristics: Dark bars against a lighter background on sides and fins; mouth with grooves at outer corners. Teeth are curved, notched on one side and serrated.

Serrations diminish in size towards the tip of the tooth. Large eyes.

Size: Young are 19 in. at birth. Largest recorded 18 ft. 4 in., but literature credits them with lengths up to 30 ft. The largest reported to Great Outdoors was 12 ft. long and weighed 1,150 lbs. It was caught by Walter Maxwell of Charlotte, N.C., at Yaupon Beach, N.C.

Color: Grey or greyish-brown with darker bars.

Range: World-wide. Greatest occurrence in the waters of the West Indies and Australia.

● **COMMON WHALER SHARK**
Galeolamna macrurus

A large shark, the Common Whaler has been known to attack humans in Australian waters. Because of its smooth skin, it is also the most commercially valuable of all sharks fished in Australia. Stingrays make up one of the major food items of this shark's diet.

Identifying Characteristics: First dorsal fin nearer tip of snout than tail fin; eyes closer to

end of snout than gills; nostrils closer to mouth than snout tip.

Size: Grows to 12 ft. A whaler this size was caught by Zane Grey in 1936, and weighed 890 pounds. Mr. Grey caught it off Batemans' Bay, New South Wales, Australia.

Color: Sandy grey above, paler below.

Range: Australia; New South Wales; Queenslond; common in lagoons at Middleton and Elizabeth Reefs.

● **TOPE SHARK**   *Galeorhinus galeus*

Also called Miller's Dog (England).

Not officially ordained a game fish, the Tope Shark is nonetheless a favorite of rod-and-reel fishermen in Britain. Once hooked, it is a good fighter, and its leaps and zig-zagging tactics make landing a real accomplishment.

Identifying Characteristics: Slender-bodied. Teeth similar in both jaws, and notched on outer margin. Lower part of the notch divided into 2 or 3 cusps. Eyes rounded.

Size: Maximum sizes for both sexes is about 6 ft. and 80 lbs. Average size 4 ft. Record Tope Shark weighed 74 lbs. 11 oz., and was caught off Caldy Island, Wales.

Color: Brownish or dusky grey above; pale below.

Range: Offshore England. Southeast coasts of Africa. Does not occur on North American east coast.

● **SOUPFIN SHARK**   *Galeorhinus zyopterus*

The Soupfin Shark received brief fame in the early 1950's as a source of both vitamin A and soup fins. It is still fished, but primarily for the latter product. The later decline in its population was probably due to the heavy fishing it once underwent. By 1970 it had returned nearly to its former level of abundance.

Identifying Characteristics: Long snout; eyes almond-shaped. Teeth in upper and lower jaws

similar. Main cusps unserrated; all teeth have deep notch on one side.

Size: Maximum length 6 ft.

Color: Grey.

Range: Western Pacific from British Columbia to Baja California; offshore Peru and Chili.

PEPPERED SHARK   *Galeus piperatus*

The Peppered Shark has one of the smallest ranges known; it has been found only in the Gulf of California. The squared-off ends of the dorsal fins, together with the restricted range, aid in identification.

Identifying Characteristics: Lining of mouth cavity dark or black; eyes elongate; young have brownish mottling or dorsal surface; tail elongate, making up almost 1/3 of total body length.

Size: Averaging 1 ft.

Color: Adults dark above, lighter below, with tiny black spots all over body.

Range: Gulf of California.

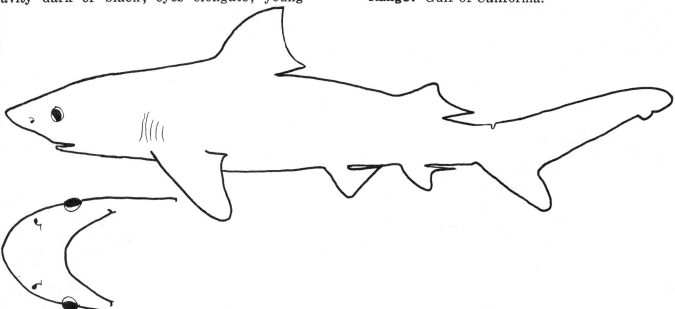

GRACEFUL SHARK

    Gillisqualus amblyrhynchoides

This shark was first described by the Australian shark expert, Gilbert Whitley, in 1934. Caught in Cape Bowling Green, Queensland, Australia, the shark has not been sighted or caught since.

Identifying Characteristics: No spiracles; folds around corners of mouth very short; nostrils nearer the eye than the tip of the rounded snout; large second dorsal; inner angle of pectoral fin farther back in relation to the first dorsal than any other Australian shark.

Size: Nearly 2 ft.

Color: Dull grey.

Range: Cape Bowling Green, Queensland, Australia.

Nurse Shark

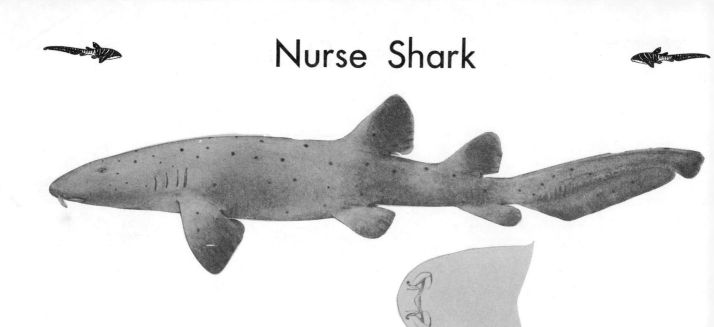

● NURSE SHARK *Ginglymostoma cirratum*

The Nurse Shark might first remind you of a catfish; this shark has fleshy barbels in front of the nostrils. It is also one of the few sharks whose skin is smooth to the touch. For the most part, it is dangerous only when harassed.

Identifying Characteristics: Barbels in front of nostrils; small eyes; nostrils connected to molth by deep groove; 4th and 5th gill slits close together. Dorsal fins almost equal in size.

Size: Reported to reach 13 ft.

Color: Yellowish to greyish-brown. Somewhat lighter below. Young often with dark spots scattered sparsely.

Range: This is the only shark of its family found in the Atlantic. It is also found in the eastern Pacific, and its range extends from the Gulf of California to Peru, and from North Carolina to South America.

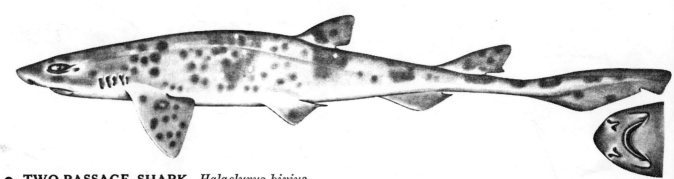

● TWO-PASSAGE SHARK *Halaelurus bivius*

Splotched, spotted and patterned like an Army camouflage technician's dream, the Two-Passage Shark resembles at first glance the Pintarroja. But in adult specimens, the head and mouth area of the Two-Passage Shark is narrower than in the Pintarroja.

Identifying Characteristics: Head short, with large mouth. Second dorsal originates over the end of the base of the anal fin. Tail short.

Size: 2 ft.

Color: Base color greyish-brown. Back splotched with indistinct crossbands. Spots both white and black on fins and back.

Range: Southern Chili, offshore.

Buerger Shark

● **BOESEMAN'S SHARK**

Halaelurus boesemani

First collected in 1841, Boeseman's Shark inhabits waters from 90 to 270 feet deep. It and the other members of its genus are separated from each other chiefly on basis of coloration.

Identifying Characteristics: Head and forward part of body wide; no ridge above eye. Snout short, and fins large.

Size: Just under 2 ft.

Color: Pale shades of yellow-brown above, with darker brown spots and saddle-like blotches. Yellow-white below. Upper surfaces of pectoral and pelvic fins with a few, nearly round black spots. Most spots smaller than pupil of eye.

Range: W. Australia, Somalia, and Gulf of Aden.

● **BUERGER SHARK**   *Halaelurus buergeri*

Restricted almost entirely to the East China Sea, the Buerger Shark is distinguished by very short and weak furrows around the mouth. It resembles closely *H. boesemani*, but its spots are fewer in number and larger.

Identifying Characteristics: Extremely short and inconspicuous furrows around corners of mouth. No bony crest above eyes. Prominant color pattern of black spots.

Size: Males a little more than 1½ ft.; females, 2 ft.

Color: Black spots, a little larger than pupil of eye, on background color of brown above, yellow below. Darker dots overlay saddle-blotches on back.

Range: Vicinity of Japan, Formosa, and Hong Kong.

● **GREY CAT SHARK** *Halaelurus canescens*

The Grey Cat Shark can be distinguished from the other cat sharks chiefly on basis of coloration. A deep-water shark, it is known only from off the coast of Peru and Chili.

Identifying Characteristics: Snout short, eyes large. Labial grooves short. Tail fin longer than other cat sharks found in same area.

Size: 2 ft. 4 in.

Color: Uniformly greyish to grey-black. Lower surface a little lighter. No well-defined spots or saddles such as found in rest of group.

Range: Depths of 2400 ft. off the coast of Peru and Chili.

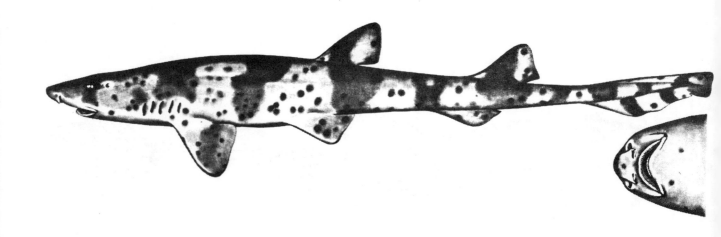

● **PINTARROJA SHARK** *Halaelurus chilensis*

The Pintarroja is one of the sharks whose adult form differs greatly from the young. Teeth in the young have three points; sexual maturity decreases the points to one, and increases tooth length. Adults are also much darker than young specimens, and show less of the blotched form so characteristic of the cat sharks.

Identifying Characteristics: Young have a row of enlarged scales on each side of the back.

Adults have modified scales above rear edge of eye.

Size: Grows to slightly less than 2 ft.

Color: Adult specimens brownish-black, with saddle-like markings and spots obscured. Young brown, with darker markings on upper surfaces.

Range: Peru and Chili.

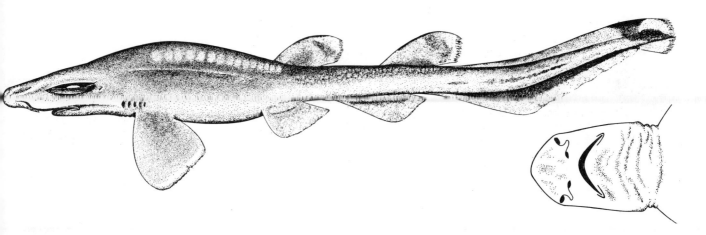

● DAWSON SHARK   *Halaelurus dawsoni*

Like the other members of the genus *Halaelurus*, the Dawson Shark is characterized by labial furrows extending around the corners of the mouth. Uniquely, it has nasal flaps that cover part of the nasal opening.

Identifying Characteristics: Broad pectoral fins; no crest above eye. Tail ¼ of total body length. Eyes fairly large and elongate.

Size: Usually between 16 and 18 in.

Color: Light brown or grey above; white or yellow-white below. Upper surfaces of fins dark near base. Specimens from Aukland Islands may have a row of white spots on each side from snout to first dorsal fin. Edges of fins light.

Range: Aukland Islands; New Zealand.

● ANDAMAN SHARK   *Halaelurus hispidus*

Since this shark was first described in 1891, 11 additional specimens have been found. All have been found in the Andaman Sea, a small area west of Thailand and east of the Andaman Islands.

Identifying Characteristics: Absence of darker saddles and spots—resembles Mud Shark in this respect. Differs from the Mud Shark in that it has small protrusions, or papillae, on the roof of the mouth. Eye length also less.

Size: To slightly less than 1 ft. The largest specimen ever found was female, and measured 11½ inches.

Color: Preserved specimens are light tan above, and yellow-white below. Fins lighter-edged. Color in life stone-grey.

Range: Andaman Sea, in depths ranging from 900 to 2200 ft.

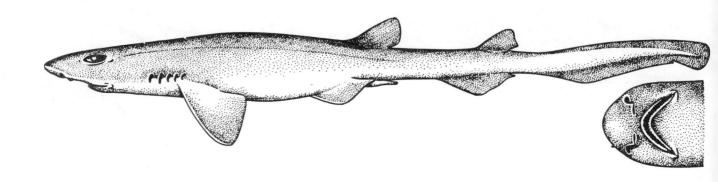

● **MUD SHARK**   *Halaelurus lutaris*

The Mud Shark can be distinguished from the other members of its genus by its lack of obvious dorsal spots or saddles.

Identifying Characteristics: Fairly even grey-brown color with no darker or lighter cross-bands. Labial furrows long. Body slender and elongated.

Size: Males average 1⅓ ft.; females a little less than 1½ ft.

Color: Brownish grey above, paler below. Some specimens may have vague saddle-blotches, but these are poorly defined and vary only slightly from the background color.

Range: Mozambique, Somalia.

● **QUAGGA SHARK**   *Halaelurus quagga*

Five male specimens of this shark have been collected since it was first described in 1899. As yet, no female has been collected or identified. Additional information solicited.

Identifying Characteristics: Evenly rounded snout tip. Distinguished from other *Halaelurus* sharks by dark bands across back.

Size: About 3 in. at birth, and probably not more than 17 in. at maturity.

Color: Dark narrow bars across back; usually 24 in number.

Range: Known only from Malabar and Somalia in depths greater than 180 ft.

EPAULETTE SHARK

Hemiscyllium ocellatum

Also called Itar Shark (North Australia).

This shark was first described by naturalists of Cook's expedition, near the present sight of Cookstown, Australia. Frequently found in shallow water, it is considered harmless and has been caught by the tail.

Size: 3 ft.

Color: Light grey-brown, with large scattered spots. One large dark spot just above and behind each pectoral fin.

Identifying Characteristics: Elongated, with tough skin of polished denticles. Said to 'grope along in a half-blind fashion' in the coral ponds it frequents.

Range: Shallow water on Great Barrier Reef; North and north-western Australia; Queensland.

SPECKLED CATSHARK

Hemiscyllium trispeculare

An elongated shark from north-western Australia, the Speckled Catshark resembles the Epaulette Shark in general body conformation except that it has more and smaller brown spots.

Identifying Characteristics: Surface covered with small brownish dots, placed closely to-gether. Snout bluntly rounded; head tapering from gills.

Size: 2 ft.

Color: Light brownish-grey with darker small brown dots. Also irregularly banded with vague vertical stripes only slightly darker than background color.

Range: North and north-western Australia; Queensland.

● **ONE-FINNED SHARK**

Heptranchias dakini

This is one of the more attractive sharks if one goes by eye color. Like the small Calf Shark, the One-Finned Shark has bright emerald green eyes. It is one of the few sharks with seven gill slits.

Identifying Characteristics: Teeth different in lower and upper jaws; teeth in upper jaws cusped; teeth in lower jaws comb-like. Tail long; head narrow, with tapering snout. Green eyes and single dorsal fin.

Size: Usually 3 ft.

Color: Grey.

Range: Australian waters, especially in New South Wales area, south of Sydney. Tasmania, Victoria, and South Australia.

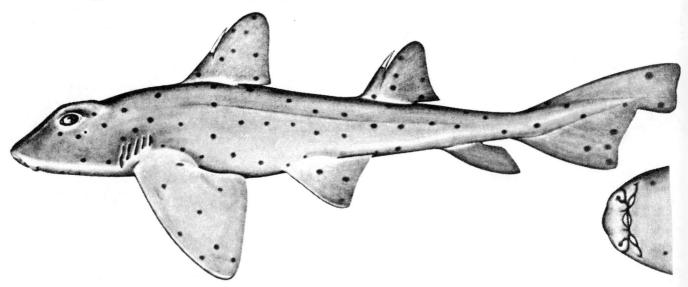

● **HORN SHARK**   *Heterodontus francisci*

Horn Sharks are members of the bullhead family. If you hook one, and reach down to bring it aboard, you will note that both dorsal fins are preceeded by a sharp spine, almost as long as the dorsal fin is high. Bullheads are like other sharks in respect to their nomenclature; scientists are currently unsure as to whether there are 2 or 3 species of bullhead sharks in the Pacific.

Identifying Characteristics: Dorsal fins preceeded by spines; nostrils connected to mouth by short groove in skin. Body frequently dotted with dark spots which fade with age. Eyes have a fleshy ridge above them.

Size: Usually less than 3 ft.

Color: Light grey to brown with darker spots

Range: Shallow and deep waters from California to Gulf of California.

● GATO SHARK   *Heterodontus quoyi*

The Gato is another bullhead shark, closely related to the Horn Shark. It can be differentiated from the Horn Shark in that its first dorsal fin originates over or behind the base of the pectoral fins. The body is also thicker, and the dorsal spines are not as large.

Identifying Characteristics: Body marked with numerous dark spots, larger and grouped more closely than in the Horn Shark. Crests above eyes low; egg case with tendrils.

Size: Maximum size unknown, but likely to be somewhat smaller than the Horn Shark. Male Gato Sharks are sexually mature at 15 in.

Color: Light grey to brown with darker spots.

Range: Known from Ecuador, Peru and the Galapagos; possibly from the Gulf of California.

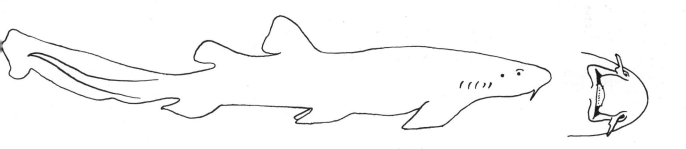

● COLCLOUGH'S SHARK
Heteroscyllium coliloughi

The position of this shark in the scientific world today is somewhat nebulous. The type specimen (the specimen from which the species was described and named) is no longer preserved. Since it was found, in 1908, no other specimens have been caught. All we have to go on is a few drawings made from the type specimen before it was destroyed.

Identifying Characteristics: Head less depressed than the Blind Shark; single barbel from each nostril; spiracle just below and behind eye; mouth located on underside of body, not projecting forward as in Blind Shark; tail and anal fins separated by short space.

Color: Pale to medium grey above, white below.

Size: 1½ ft.

Range: Single specimen was caught off southern Queensland, Australia.

● **SIXGILL SHARK**   *Hexanchus griseus*

It is a fairly reliable fact among sharks that if the dorsal fin is exactly ¼ the body length in the young shark, then this proportion will hold true for adult sharks as well. The Hexanid sharks don't adhere to this rule, however, and this makes the already tricky business of shark identification even trickier. But logically, the Sixgill Shark has exactly that—six pairs of gills (most sharks have 5).

Identifying Characteristics: Six pairs of gills; tail elongated; single dorsal fin; snout almost squared off at the tip, but becoming more pointed as the shark grows to a larger size. Tail 1/3 of total body length. Large eyes.

Size: 20 in. at birth, maturing to a length of 15 ft. Sexually mature at 6 to 7 ft.

Color: Grey.

Range: Cool waters from British Columbia to southern California; Hawaiian Islands. The young may be found in San Francisco Bay and Puget Sound. Abundant off the north coast of Cuba.

● **CALF SHARK**   *Hexanchus vitulus*

Bright green eyes mark the Calf Shark, the latest addition to the cowshark family.

Identifying Characteristics: Proportionally larger eyes and longer snout than the Sixgill Shark. Head abruptly rounded in front of nostrils. 6 gill slits. Pectorals broad and short. Single dorsal fins set far back on upper side. Upper lobe of tail notched.

Size: Sexually mature at 5½ ft. Maximum length probably not more than 7 ft. 2½ in.

Color: Grey all over, with upper side a shade darker than underside.

Range: Common in Florida-Gulf of Mexico region. May extend to all waters of tropical and subtropical Atlantic, the Mediterrenean, Indian and west Pacific Oceans.

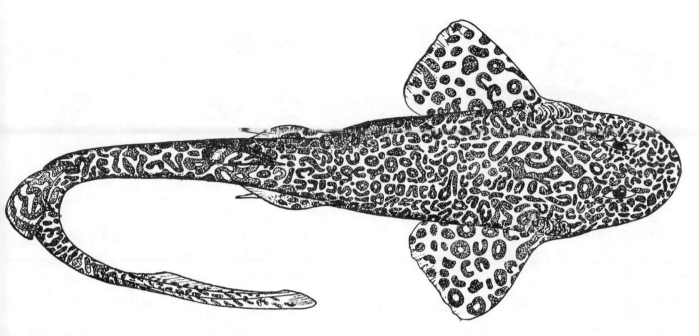

● IZAK SHARK   *Holohalaelurus regani*

Resembling at first the Wobbegong, the Izak Shark differs in the absence of snout barbels, longer tail, and smaller anal fins.

Identifying Characteristics: Head broad and depressed. Mottled markings become more reticulated with age and increased size.

Size: To 4 ft., but more commonly about 2.

Color: Brownish-grey, with white spots or reticulations.

Range: Commonly found in Indo-Pacific area.

● IAGO SHARK   *Iago omanensis*

The Iago Shark, the only member of a genus created especially for it, was named after the villan of Shakespeare's *Otello*. It differs from the other carcharhinid sharks in the forward location of the first dorsal fin.

Identifying Characteristics: Head flattened; adults lack lower lobe of tail. Ridge between dorsal fins; crest above eye.

Size: Males usually up to about 15 in.; females to 23 in.

Color: Brownish or greyish above; lighter below.

Range: North Arabian Sea, and possibly Red Sea.

● **CIGAR SHARK**   *Isistius brasiliensis*

The Cigar Shark is the most brilliantly luminous shark of the Squalidae, a family known for its bioluminescent members.

Identifying Characteristics: Elongate body. Dark collar around neck behind gill slits; dorsal fins located far back on body. Base of second dorsal fin slightly longer than base of first dorsal. Pectoral fins too small and rounded to be used as planing mechanism.

Size: Reaches a maximum of about 1½ ft.

Range: Tropical and subtropical belts of all seas, in midwater areas.

Color: Grey, with rear edges of pectoral and dorsal fins white. Dark ring around neck.

● **MAKO SHARK**   *Isurus oxyrinchus*

Also called the Bonito Shark and Atlantic Mako.

The Mako Shark is highly prized for its game-fish qualities; when hooked, it puts up a spectacular struggle, and is one of the few sharks recognized by the International Game Fish Association as a true game fish. Known attacker.

Identifying Characteristics: Slender body, crescent-shaped tail; unserrated teeth; long gill slits.

Size: 12 ft. The largest reported to Great Outdoors was 12 ft. 2 in. long, and weighed 1061 lbs. It was caught by Richard Webster off Rockport, Mass.

Color: Dark blue-grey, white below.

Range: Tropical and warm-temperate Atlantic; eastern Pacific.

GULF CATSHARK   *Junerus vincenti*

The egg-case of the Gulf Catshark is remarkable in its mode of attachment to seaweed or other support. It is covered with fine threads or filaments that serve to anchor the eggcase securely.

Identifying Characteristics: Elongate form; pelvic fins of males connected behind the claspers; first dorsal originates over posterior base of pelvic fin; second dorsal originates over posterior base of anal fin.

Size: 2 ft.

Color: Dark brown with white spots. Underside lighter and not spotted.

Range: South and western Australia.

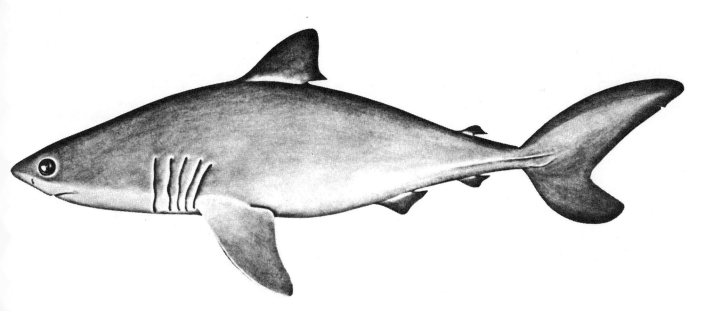

SALMON SHARK   *Lamna ditropis*

The Salmon Shark is a member of the mackerel shark family. Like the other sharks in the family, it is characterized by the ridge, or keel, on each side of the rear body leading to the tail. In addition, though, the Salmon Shark has a second smaller keel.

Identifying Characteristics: Primary and secondary caudal keels; first dorsal located at about body midpoint; tail large and fairly wide; second dorsal small.

Size: To 10 ft.

Color: Dark grey, lighter below. Large specimens may have dark blotches on undersides.

Range: North Pacific area, in both inshore and offshore waters.

Porbeagle Shark

● PORBEAGLE   *Lamna nasus*

The Porbeagle Shark is another shark that mascarades as swordfish steaks. It is found in both oceans, primarily in deep waters.

Identifying Characteristics: Body leading into tail flattened; two keels on tail; tail crescent-shaped; teeth usually with small secondary cusp on each side of the main cusp.

Size: 10 ft.

Color: Dark bluish grey on upper surface, white below.

Range: Southern Pacific waters, both eastern and western areas. Northern Atlantic.

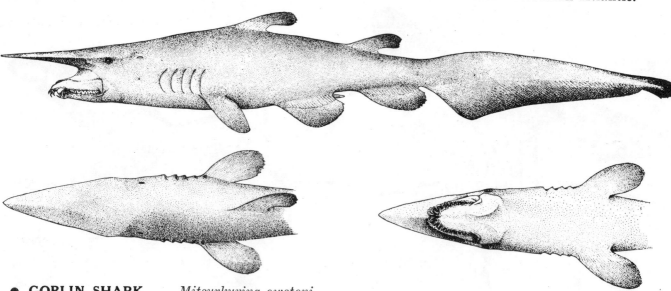

● GOBLIN SHARK   *Mitsurkurina owstoni*

Also called Elfin Shark.

The Goblin Shark is the only living representative of the family Scapanorhynchidae. Rarely caught, it is thought to be a bottom-feeder, eating the shellfish it catches there. This unusual shark is characterized by the exaggerated snout development. Like all sharks, the Goblin Shark protrudes its mouth forward to feed, adding to the bizarre appearance.

Identifying Characteristics: Snout extends far beyond mouth. Small, stubby dorsal fins. Small pectoral fins. Tail roughly 1/3 of total body length. Upper portion of tail fleshy and thick.

Size: Known to reach 14′, but usually about 8′

Color: Dark shades of brown to grey.

Range: Pacific Ocean—the "Black Current" or Gulf Stream off Japan.

Grey Smoothhound

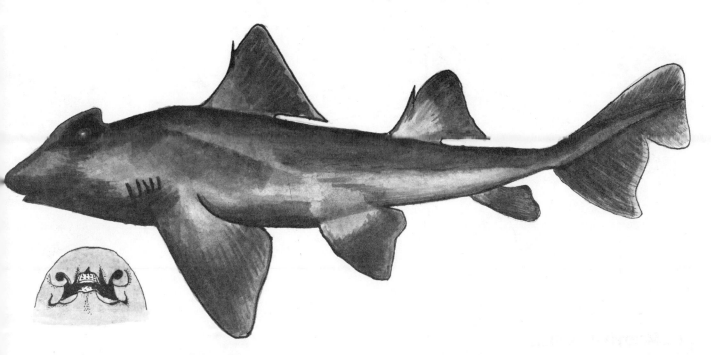

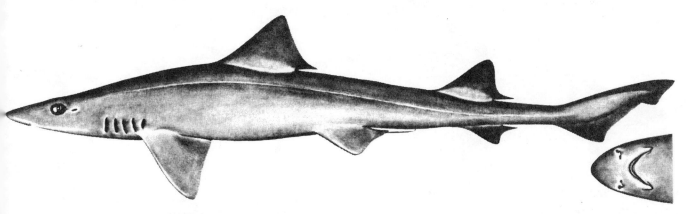

● **CRESTED PORT JACKSON SHARK**
Molochophrys galeatus

The Crested Port Jackson Shark, like the Hammerhead sharks, chooses what might ordinarilly be considered uncomfortable items for its diet. In this case, one of the staple foods is purple sea urchins. As a result, the skin and teeth are often stained a reddish-brown.

Identifying Characteristics: Teeth rounded grinders; ridges over each eye have a distinct elevated rear edge. Dorsal fins high and resemble triangular flags, stuck by one lower corner to body.

Size: 4 ft.

Color: Light brown, sometimes with reddish stain.

Range: Australia, Queensland and New South Wales. Possibly Tasmania.

● **GREY SMOOTHHOUND SHARK**
Mustelus californicus

The teeth of the Grey Smoothhound are rounded, and fit together much like bricks in pavement. Such teeth are usually used for grinding, as in a diet of crustaceans or molluscs.

Identifying Characteristics: Head tapering from spiracles, snout slightly rounded but still distinctly pointed; lateral line apparent but without white line; teeth rounded.

Size: To slightly more than 3½ ft.

Color: Medium grey.

Range: Close to shore, from the Gulf of California to central California.

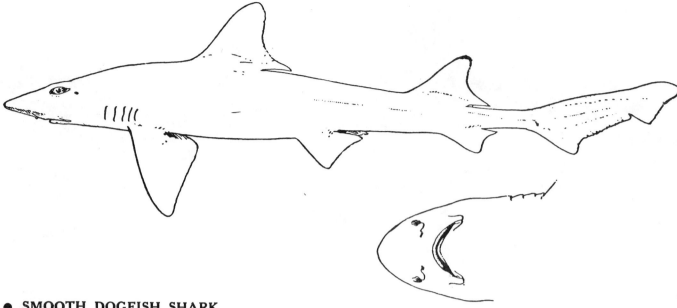

● SMOOTH DOGFISH SHARK
Mustelus canis

Like the fabled swallows of Capistrano, the Smooth Dogfish appears each spring for nesting. Somewhat less romantic than the swallows, however, their nesting site is the entrance to Long Island Sound.

Identifying Characteristics: Dorsal fins of nearly same size; minute, pavement-like teeth; fairly large eyes.

Size: 5 ft.

Color: Shades of grey and brown above, shading in pale grey or white below.

Range: Northern Atlantic.

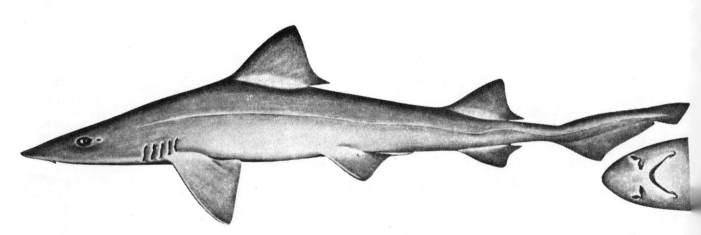

● SHARPTOOTHED SMOOTHHOUND SHARK
Mustelus dorsalis

The Sharptoothed Smoothhound is one of the smaller, lesser-known smoothhounds. Like most of the members of its family, it's an inshore species, and stays close to the ocean bottom.

Identifying Characteristics: Snout pointed and long; blunted at the extreme tip; nostrils close to mouth; eyes small; pectorals broad.

Size: Slightly less than 20 inches.

Color: Brown or grey.

Range: Panama, Gulf of California, Costa Rica and Peru.

44

SICKLEFIN SMOOTHHOUND SHARK
Mustelus lunulatus

The curved arcs of the dorsal fins identify the Sicklefin Smoothhound. Like the Grey Smoothhound, the Sicklefin feeds on crustaceans and molluscs it crushes with its pavement-like teeth.

Identifying Characteristics: Head narrow, snout long; eyes large; anal fin half the size of the second dorsal.

Size: Maximum size appears to be about 5 ft.

Color: Brownish-grey.

Range: Northern Mexico to Central America.

TOLLO SHARK   *Mustelus mento*

The Tollo Shark is one of the few sharks whose lateral line is clearly indicated by a narrow band of white dots and lines. Armed with a rather unimpressive set of rounded teeth lacking cusps, it is an inshore species.

Identifying Characteristics: Lateral line marked with white dots or lines; lower lobe of tail small; large eyes.

Size: Probably to slightly more than 4 ft.

Color: Base color or grey, with dark transverse bars or white flecks on younger specimens. Older specimens grey, with or without white flecks.

Range: Inshore Chili and Peru.

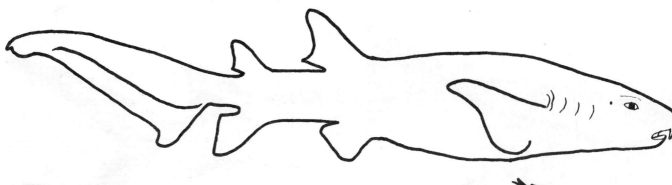

● **TAWNY SHARK**

Nebrodes concolor ogilbyi

Also called the "Madam X" Shark.

Scientists for a long time have doubted the existance of this shark. It's a shark reputed to spurt water from the mouth at fishermen when hauled to the surface, and at the same time giving "coughing grunt". The doubt is understandable. Yet this crazy shark apparently does exist.

Identifying Characteristics: Minute spiracles; fourth and fifth gill slits close together; coarse denticles on skin; eyes small; spurts water from mouth; vocalizes.

Size: Probably more than 3 ft., but specimens are rare in collections.

Color: Sandy brown or tawny.

Range: Queensland, Australia, and possibly Tonga.

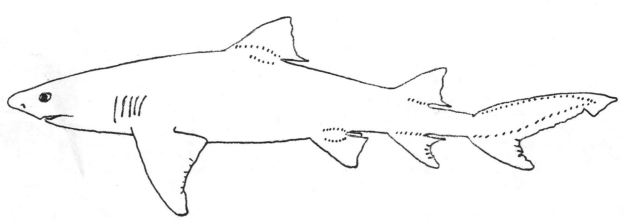

● **LEMON SHARK**   *Negaprion brevirostris*

This is the only shark whose actual tooth-replacement rate has been measured. Young Lemon Sharks replace teeth in the upper jaw every 7.8 days, and teeth in the lower jaw every 8.2 days. The Lemon Shark, however, is primarily known for its yellow-brown coloration and its tendency to attack humans.

Identifying Characteristics: Second and first dorsal fins nearly identical in size. Snout short and broad.

Size: Twenty-five inches at birth, growing to a maximum of 11 ft. The largest reported to Great Outdoors (hooked by Larry Dunston of Elizabeth, N.J.) was 9 ft. 2 in. long and weighed 352 lbs.

Color: Frequently yellow-brown above, shading to white or yellow below. Also occurs in all shades of grey, ranging to blue-grey.

Range: World-wide in temperate western Atlantic waters, the south Pacific, and the Indian Ocean. Particularly common in the West Indies. An inshore species.

● **TRIBURON AMARILLO** *Negaprion fronto*

The Amarillo Shark is most easily recognized by the two dorsal fins; the second is nearly as large as the first. It is well known to the tuna-fishing industry in the Pacific; tuna is one of its favorite foods.

Identifying Characteristics: Teeth of both jaws unserrated; snout blunt; small eyes; no folds at corner of mouth. Dorsal fins nearly the same size.

Size: Grows to 10 ft.

Color: Varying shades of brown to grey.

Range: Warm inshore waters of the eastern Pacific, from the Gulf of California to Peru.

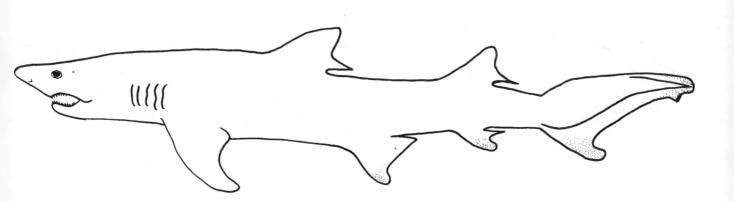

● **SHARP-TOOTHED SHARK**
Negaprion queenslandicus

The coloration of the Sharp-toothed Shark reminds one of a strawberry confection—all shades of light and dark brown, pink, and white. And, in keeping with the innocuous color combination, this large shark is considered harmless.

Identifying Characteristics: Elongate body, with heavy jaw area; snout short and broad, with crescent-shaped mouth; second dorsal larger than anal; and originating slightly ahead of it.

Size: Over 6 ft.

Color: Light to pale brown above, white below. Fins a darker shade of brown, with areas of pink and grey towards tip.

Range: Australia; north Australia to Queensland.

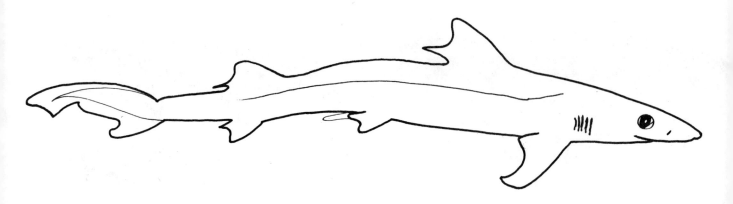

● **WEASEL SHARK**   *Negogaleus microstoma*

Named for its slender and wiry body, the Weasel Shark has an extraordinarily long caudal peduncle—the area between the second dorsal fin and the tail.

Identifying Characteristics: Long caudal peduncle; small pectoral fins; large eyes; nictitating membrane present; body elongate.

Size: To slightly less than 3 ft.

Color: Silver-grey above with some iridescence. White below.

Range: Australia; Queensland.

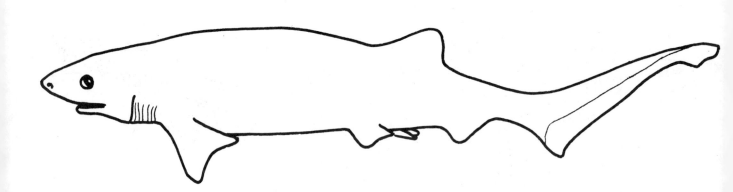

● **TUATINI SHARK**
                    Notorhynchus cepedianus

Named by the Maoris, the teeth of this shark were once used to make war weapons, *oripi tuatini*. The teeth were mounted along the edges of spear shafts, creating a weapon rather awesome in its ability to do damage.

Identifying Characteristics: Single dorsal fin; seven gill slits; head broad, with broadly rounded snout.

Size: To slightly more than 9½ ft.

Color: Upper surface sandy-grey, with scattered black and white spots, paler below.

Range: New Zealand (not looked upon as dangerous in this area), South Australia (but considered harmful here), Tasmania, New South Wales, and Victoria

 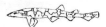

● SEVENGILL SHARK
Notorhynchus maculatus

Aside from having one more gill slit than the Sixgill Shark, the Sevengill Shark has a more broadly rounded snout. It occurs in almost the same geographical area as the sixgill, but as far as has been determined, has not been reported from the warmer waters.

Identifying Characteristics: Snout broadly rounded; single dorsal fin. Upper surface usually marked with dark and/or light spots. Such spots smaller than the eye.

Size: Grows to 8½ ft.

Color: Dark grey.

Range: Cooler waters from British Columbia to Chili.

● PACIFIC SAND SHARK *Odontaspis ferox*

Sometimes grouped with the Carcharinid sharks, the sand sharks contain only a single genus, and fewer than 10 species. This particular sand shark, the Pacific Sand Shark, is notable because it is the only member of its genus found in the eastern Pacific.

Identifying Characteristics: Fifth gill opening behind origin of pectoral fins; both second dorsal and anal fins almost as large as first dorsal; stout body with rounded belly.

Size: To about 10 ft., but more commonly about 6 ft.

Color: Medium to dark grey.

Range: Southern California, and perhaps as far south as the Gulf of California.

● ATLANTIC SAND SHARK
Odontaspis taurus

Also called Grey Nurse Shark (Australia), Brown Shark (South America) and Ragged Tooth Shark (South Africa).

This is one of the sharks whose young are cannibals even before they are born. One baby shark in each oviduct will hatch before any of the others, and will feed upon them. Hence, only two sand sharks are born each time.

Identifying Characteristics: Pointed snout with long, slender teeth protruding from mouth; enlarged caudal lobe (helps with quick identification).

Size: 10½ ft., 400 lbs.

Color: Grey-brown above, and grey-white below. Back half of body may be peppered with fairly large, dark spots.

Range: Western Atlantic from the Gulf of Maine to Florida and south Brazil. May also be found in the Mediterranean, tropical West Africa, and the Canary Islands.

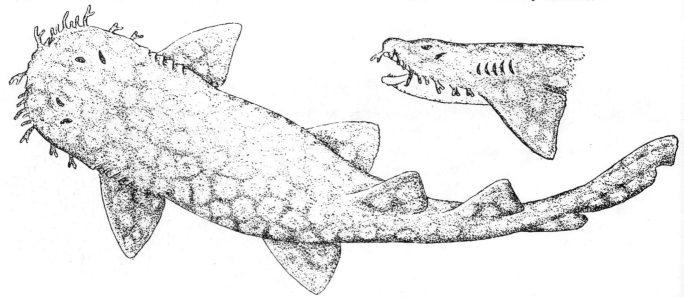

● WOBBEGONG   Orectolobus maculatus

The Wobbegong, named by the Australian aborigines, is a beautifully patterned and marked shark. Mouth fringed with barbels, this shark spends its time lying amoung the weeds and rocks of the ocean botom.

Identifying Characteristics: Fringe of barbels, rather like a mustache, around mouth. Body heavy and wide, tapering rapidly after anal fins to tail.

Size: To 10½ ft.

Color: Dark grey-brown with cream semicircles and spots distributed over body. Spots usually a little larger than eye.

Range: Indo-Pacific. Especially common around Australia.

● **CARPET SHARK**   *Orectolobus ornatus*

Also called Banded Wobbegong (Australia).

The Carpet Shark is a night-feeding shark, and spends its days resting quietly on the ocean bottom. It has been reported as attacking waders and fishermen, but probably it is only retaliating for being stepped on.

Identifying Characteristics: Large spiracles; deep groove on lower lip (not as long as in the Blind Shark); thin barbels on each side of head.

Size: 7 ft.

Color: Marbled dark brown and white; darker brown bars at intervals across body marked with white or pale ocelli or "eye-spots"; white bars marked with brown ocelli.

Range: Eastern coast of Australia, from New Guinea to Victoria, and probably Tasmania.

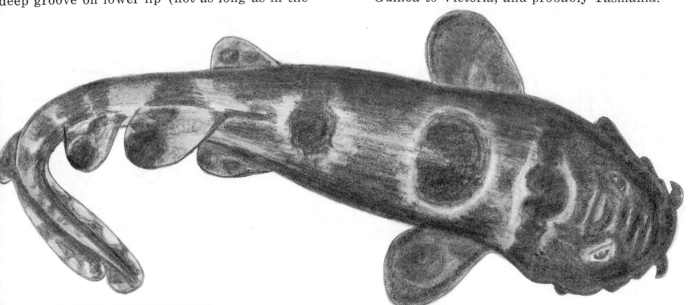

● **NORTHERN WOBBEGONG**
   Orectolobus wardi

The smooth-backed Northern Wobbegong is perhaps most easily distinguished from its close relative, the Cobbler Carpet shark, by its rounded, short barbels, and the lack of tubercules (small bumps) on its back.

Identifying Characteristics: Nasal and skin barbels short and blunt; 3 large dark circles on back; skin of head somewhat wrinkled.

Size: Usually 18 in.

Color: Background color yellow-grey, back with greater grey tones than lower side; 3 large spots on back between eyes and first dorsal, continuing around into encircling dark bands; tail with 3 dark bands, one each at the base of both dorsal and anal fins.

Range: North and northeastern Australia.

● **COLLARED CATSHARK**

Parascyllium collare

Distinctly patterned with a combination of dark rings and blackish spots, the Collared Catshark has not been known to venture into water less than 60 ft. deep.

Identifying Characteristics: Entire anal fin base ahead of second dorsal fin; fusiform body; first dorsal originates behind pelvic fins.

Size: 34 inches.

Color: Brown with large dark spots and vertical bands around body. Band behind eyes and before pectoral fins darker than other bands, forming a collar.

Range: Southern Australia and Tasmania.

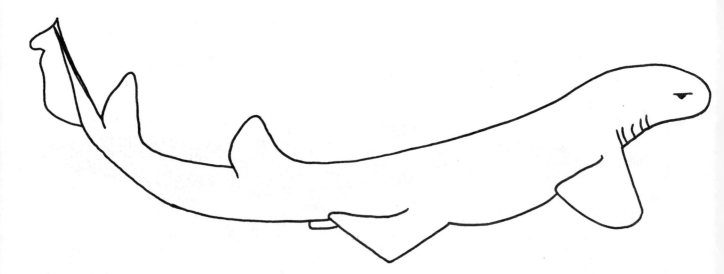

● **RUSTY CATSHARK**

Parascyllium ferrugineum

The Rusty Catshark has the elongated body form typical of the catshark family. The large fins and black spots serve to separate it from the rest of the catsharks. Indistinct dark crossbands begin at nape level and continue to tail tip. Nape crossband has three similar dark spots on each side.

Identifying Characteristics: Head broad, with broadly rounded snout; fins larger than Collared Catshark.

Size: 2½ ft.

Color: Greyish brown with brown spots.

Range: Victoria, South Australia, and South-western Australia, usually in depths of 75 ft.

● **TASMANIAN SPOTTED CATSHARK**
  Parascyllium multimaculatum

Known only from a single specimen collected in Tasmania in 1934, this shark is characterized by the pattern of small dots and the position of the first dorsal.

Identifying Characteristics: First dorsal located behind midpoint of total length. Majority of body bulk in front of first dorsal. Small tail.

Size: Slightly less than 30 inches.

Color: General color pale grey, with brownish cast. Underside almost white. Ten vague bars of rusty brown on sides. Small dark spots on sides and back.

Range: Northern Tasmania.

● **VARIED CATSHARK**
  Parascyllium variolatum

Differs from the Collared Catshark in having greater length between anal fin and first dorsal fin. Broad dark band over gill area dotted with spots, giving the appearance of a jewelled collar.

Identifying Characteristics: Broad black-brown collar, with white spots. Fins spotted with dark blotches; dark body clouded with white splotches.

Size: 3 feet.

Color: Dark brown with white and black-brown spots.

Range: Victoria, Tasmania, South Australia, and southwestern Australia. Known to occur in depths of 360 feet.

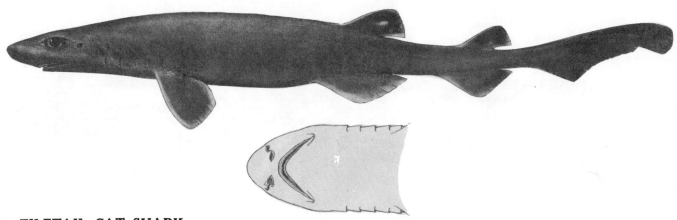

● **FILETAIL CAT SHARK**
Parmaturus xaniurus

This is another member of the catshark family whose identification is verified by the color of the mouth lining. The Peppered Shark has a dark lining in the mouth; the Filetail Cat Shark has a white lining.

Identifying Characteristics: Head broad, tapering foreword. Mouth large. Modified scales on upper edge of caudal fin.

Size: Proabably less than 1½ ft.

Color: Dark shades of brown-black; lower surface may be slightly lighter. Fins blotched and white-bordered.

Range: Western Pacific, from central California to Gulf of California.

● **BLUE SHARK**   *Prionace glauca*

Also called Blue Pointer (Australia).

Color is the most striking thing about the Blue Shark. A brilliant blue above, shading to white below, this is one of the most common of the large oceanic sharks. Several reports credit the Blue Shark with both an insensitivity to pain and a willingness to eat almost anything. "Anything" in this case, extends to old boots, blocks of wood, and garbage thrown from passing ships. It also includes people.

Identifying Characteristics: Blue above, paling to white below; long, sickle-shaped pectoral fins; long pointed snout. First dorsal fin set far back on head.

Size: Largest ever recorded 12 ft. 7 in. Weight of a 9 ft. specimen is about 235 lbs.; this compares with a 478-lb. Blue Shark hooked by Bobby Kentrolis of Wilmington, N.C. No length recorded for this particular record, however.

Color: Blue above, white below. The blue color fades rapidly with death.

Range: All temperate and tropical seas of the world.

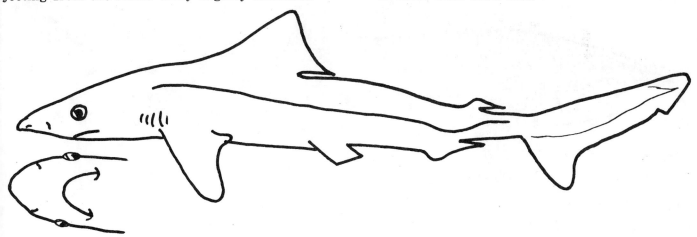

● SCHROEDER'S SAW SHARK
Pristiophorus schroederi

The saw sharks belong to a primitive family representing the transition between sharks and rays. The most noticeable item about this particular shark is the saw-like extension of the snout. It looks much like a sawfish at first glance, but the gill slits of the saw shark are located on the *sides* of the head, and the pectoral fins are joined to the body *behind* the gill slits.

Identifying Characteristics: Snout modified into long flat blade, set sideways, with teeth projecting from the sides. Body slightly flattened from top to bottom, head considerably flattened. Pair of barbels located about halfway down the length of the saw.

Size: To 5 ft.

Color: Light grey above, whitish below. A brownish stripe on each side of the saw.

Range: Bahaman banks, and Santaren Channel off the southeast coast of Florida. Other members of this little-known family are found near Japan, southeast Africa and Australia. This family is probably widely distributed in depths of more than 1200 feet.

● TAYLOR'S SHARK   *Protozygaena taylori*

The lateral line of Taylor's Shark takes a sudden dip between the second dorsal and anal fins. The clear junction between the colors of the upper and lower surfaces is also another identifying feature of this fairly common Australian shark.

Identifying Characteristics: Lateral line dips between second dorsal and anal fins; no spiracle; short snout; second dorsal and anal fins both low in profile, with anal fin less than twice the length of the second dorsal.

Size: Slightly less than 3 ft.

Color: Upper surfaces blue-grey, contrasting sharply with pale underside.

Range: Australia, from the Northern Territory to Queensland.

False Catshark

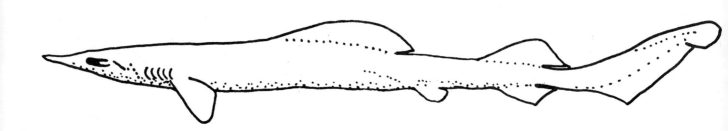

● **FALSE CATSHARK** *Pseudotrakis microdon*

This is one of the rarer sharks. Only about 12 specimens have been caught or washed ashore. It appears to be a deep-water shark, and can be readily identified by the great length of its dorsal fin.

Identifying Characteristics: Base of first dorsal very long, equal to about ¼ of total body length.

Size: Perhaps larger than 9 ft. 8 in. This record size has held since 1883, when a False Cat-

shark of this size washed ashore on Long Island. Even the length of full-term young is unknown; one captured female yielded embryos 2 ft. 9 in. in length.

Color: Uniformly dark brownish-grey.

Range: Both sides of the Atlantic. Specimens have been taken off Spain, Portugal, Iceland, New York and New Jersey.

● **WHALE SHARK** *Rhincodon typus*

The Whale Shark is one of the largest of all the sharks. Despite its enormous size, it is a placid and inoffensive animal. It feeds on plankton as well as small fishes and squid it finds as it cruises along the surface. Its size and the distinctive white-on-grey pattern make identification easy.

Identifying Characteristics: Large size (up to 45 ft.). Body with longitudinal ridges extending from top of head to base of tail.

Size: To 45 ft. The heaviest weight ever recorded was 26,594 pounds for a 38-ft. specimen caught off Knight's Key, Florida, in 1912. Young are about 15 inches on hatching.

Color: Grey with contrasting white vertical stripes and rows of dots.

Range: Tropical water all over the world. May stray into temperate zones.

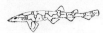

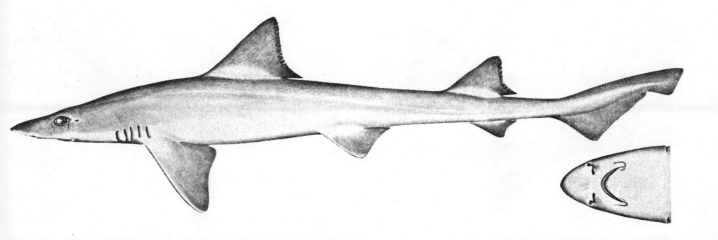

● BROWN SMOOTHHOUND SHARK
Rhinotriacis henlei

The rear margins of both the dorsal fins of the Brown Smoothhound are frayed and thin. In this respect it resembles the heavier carcharhinid shark, the Cuero Duro. There are two fin characteristics of the Cuero Duro that differ from the Smoothhound, however; only first dorsal of the Cuero Duro is tattered, and the rear margin of its anal fin is deeply indented.

Identifying Characteristics: Pointed snout; tail fin without distinct lower lobe; rear margins of both dorsals tattered and thin; head depressed.

Size: 3 ft.

Color: Brown or grey.

Range: California to Central America.

● PACIFIC SHARPNOSE SHARK
Rhizoprionodon longurio

As the common name implies, the Pacific Sharpnose is most readily identified on the basis of its sharply pointed nose. The body is more streamlined than in other sharks, with lower dorsal fins and the tail tip horizontal to the body.

Identifying Characteristics: Teeth in both jaws unserrated, but with a deep notch on one side.

Second dorsal originates farther back than does anal fin. Pointed snout.

Size: Largest recorded 3 ft. 8 in.

Color: Medium grey to brown.

Range: Temperate and tropical coastal Pacific waters from southern California to Peru.

● ATLANTIC SHARPNOSE SHARK
Rhizoprionodon terranovae

The Atlantic Sharpnose Shark differs from its close relative, the Finetooth Shark, in the shape of the teeth and the origin of the anal fin directly under the second dorsal.

Identifying Characteristics: Dorsal fin originates over middle of pectoral fins. Well-developed furrows extend from corners of the mouth almost to the nostrils. Teeth smooth-edged, and similar in both jaws.

Size: Averages about 3 ft.

Color: Brownish to olive-grey; paler below.

Range: Western north Atlantic.

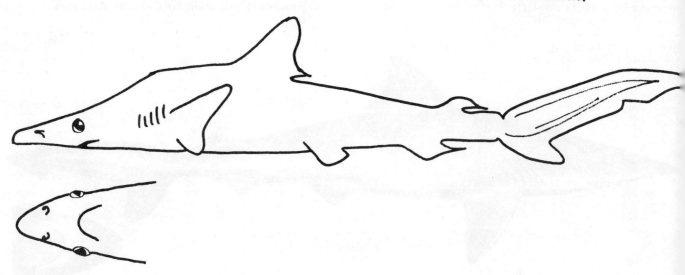

● SLENDER DOG SHARK
Scolionodon jordani

Also called Jordan's Dog Shark (Australia).

The flat lower surface and humped back of the Slender Dog Shark give a good clue to its identity. It is a inshore species, rarly venturing in depths of more than 150 ft.

Identifying Characteristics: Teeth without serrations; height of first dorsal greater than length; origin of second dorsal behind origin of anal fin.

Size: 3 ft.

Color: Shades of dark blue-grey above, shading to grey below. Pectoral and pelvic fins edged with grey.

Range: Australia; Queensland.

58

# Greenland Shark

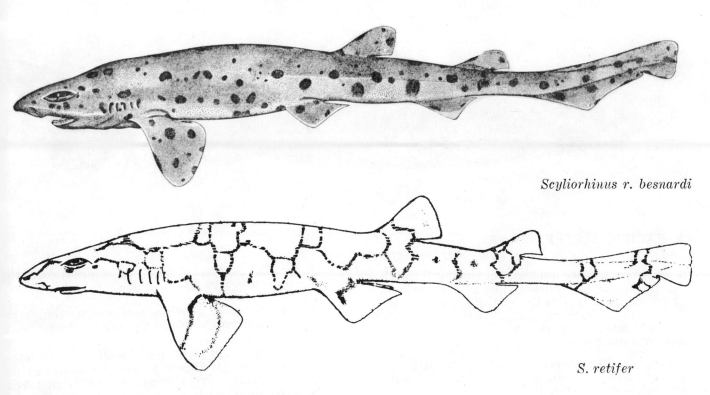

Scyliorhinus r. besnardi

S. retifer

● **CHAIN DOGFISH** *Scyliorhinus retifer*

One of the cool-water cat sharks, the Chain Dogfish is most easily identified by the dark webbing pattern on its back and sides. Like the other members of its family, it only rarely ventures into the warmer shoal areas.

Identifying Characteristics: Dorsal and lateral surfaces covered with irregular black webbing pattern, on top of base color. First dorsal located in back of pelvic fins.

Size: 2½ ft.

Color: Dark reddish brown on upper surfaces, fading to a yellowish shade below. Chainlike pattern black. *Besnardi* subspecies patterned with dark spots instead of webbing pattern.

Range: Northern western Atlantic coast from New York to North Carolina.

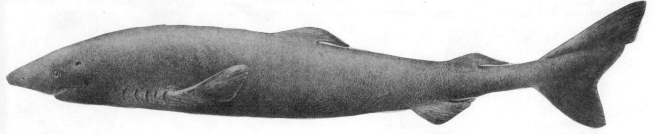

● **GREENLAND SHARK**
Somniosis microcephalus

The Greenland Shark presents a bit of a puzzle. It is known to be a lethargic shark, and spends a great deal of its time lying on the bottom. The confusion begins when you try to explain why Greenland Sharks have been caught with seals and even whole reindeer in their stomachs! How such a sluggish shark manages to catch such prey is a mystery those who study sharks would like very much to have cleared up.

Identifying Characteristics: No anal fin or dorsal spines. Second dorsal originates opposite back edge of pectoral fins.

Size: Largest on record 24 ft. and 2000 pounds.

Color: Brown to grey to black all over. Sometimes back and sides dotted or banded with darker bands or whitish spots.

Range: Western Atlantic waters along Greenland and Labrador, rarely as far south as New England.

Pacific Sleeper

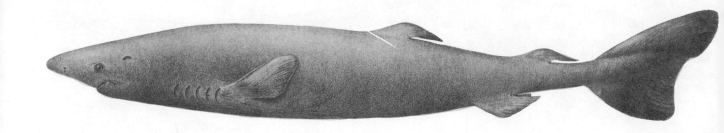

● PACIFIC SLEEPER SHARK
Somniosus pacificus

If you expect to see a dorsal fin knifing through the water as this shark swims at the surface, you'll be disappointed. The Pacific Sleeper Shark has an extremely small first dorsal fin, located midway between the pectoral and second dorsal fins.

Identifying Characteristics: All fins small; eyes small; large individuals very stout, with well-formed lower lobe of tail.

Size: To at least 13 ft. A related Atlantic species grows to 20 ft.

Color: Ash-grey above, sometimes mottled with white. Not much lighter below.

Range: Arctic waters, occasionally as far southward as north California. On the western side of the Pacific, from Japan to the Bering Sea and south Alaska.

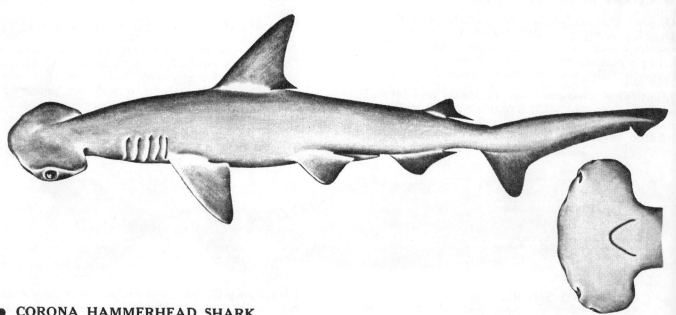

● CORONA HAMMERHEAD SHARK
Sphyrna corona

The head shape of the Corona Hammerhead places it midway between the Bonnethead and Scoophead. To be technical, the Corona Hammerhead can be identified if the distance between the front edge of the head and the mouth is less than 2/5 the greatest width of the head.

Identifying Characteristics: Head bulging forward between eyes to form shallow arc; mid-

line of head may have shallow indentation; shallow pit on each side of body, just before origin of tail.

Size: Small; rarely exceeding 3 ft.

Color: Dark grey-brown, paler below.

Range: Western coast of South America northward to southern Mexico.

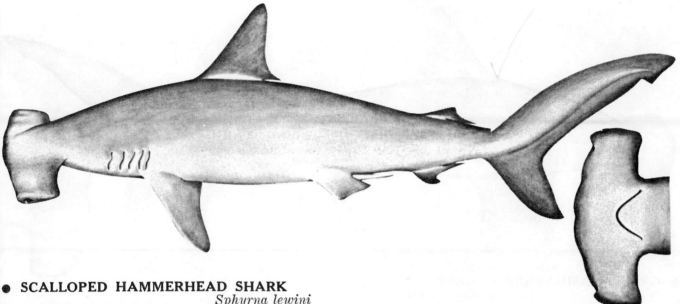

● SCALLOPED HAMMERHEAD SHARK
Sphyrna lewini

Stingrays are one of the favorite foods of the Scalloped Hammerhead. One large specimen was found to have more than 50 stingray barbs imbedded around his mouth.

Identifying Characteristics: Head indented at midline much like the Great Hammerhead, but the front edge of head more rounded. Teeth have smooth edges.

Size: To 13 ft.

Color: Pale grey on upper surfaces, paler below. Underside of pectorals often edged in black.

Range: Tropical and warm waters of both the Atlantic and Pacific.

● SCOOPHEAD SHARK   *Sphyrna media*

Possessing a wide head with an almost-straight front edge, the Scoophead is one of the smallest Hammerheads. Its general body conformation is much stockier than the other species, and the tail lobe is fleshier.

Identifying Characteristics: Front margin on wide head almost straight. First dorsal not as high or arched as in Scalloped Hammerhead.

Size: Grows to a maximum of 5 ft.

Color: Dark grey above, paler below.

Range: South from the Gulf of California to Peru and Ecuador.

● **GREAT HAMMERHEAD SHARK**
Sphyrna mokarran

The shape of the hammer is the key to distinguishing the species of hammerheads. One of the largest of the hammerheads, the Great Hammerhead, has a hammer almost rectangular in shape. The hammer also is indented at the center, just in front of the mouth.

Identifying Characteristics: Head indented at midline; first dorsal slanted backwards; teeth serrated; tail long.

Size: The largest of the hammerheads, the Great Hammerhead has been recorded at an impressive length of 18 ft. 4 in.

Color: Olive-brown above, paler below.

Range: All oceans in tropical and subtropical waters.

● **BONNETHEAD SHARK**   *Sphyrna tiburo*

The head of the Bonnethead is almost a perfect semicircle. The shovel-like shape of the head explains another common name for this shark —the Shovelhead.

Identifying Characteristics: Shovel-shaped hammer; first dorsal high and narrow; may be found in groups or large swarms; found chiefly in shallow water.

Size: To 6 ft.

Color: Greyish-brown or grey above, shading to paler grey or white below.

Range: Warm to tropical waters of both oceans.

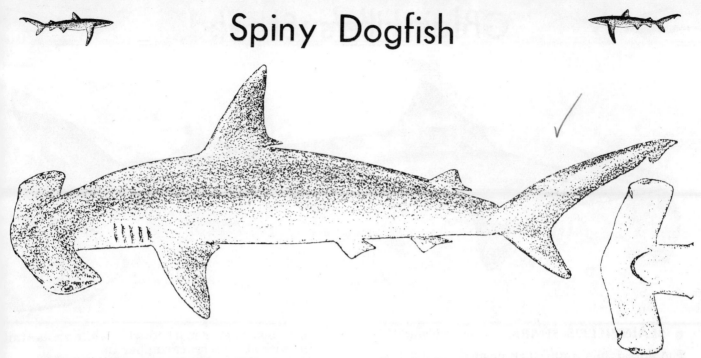

● SMOOTH HAMMERHEAD SHARK
Sphyrna zygaena

Also known as Balance Fish (Australia) and Cornuda (West Africa).

Only one of nine species of hammerhead sharks, the Smooth Hammerhead has a smooth, rounded hammer. Known to attack humans, it is also a good fighter on rod and reel.

Identifying Characteristics: Hammer rounded at midline; rear tip of second dorsal twice longer than high; deep notch and hammer in front of each nostril.

Size: Average length 6 ft. The record 13 ft., 725 pounds. This compares with the largest reported to Great Outdoors of 710 pounds (no length given). This shark was caught by Robert Keller of Cleveland, Ohio, off Jeanette's Fishing Pier, Nagshead, N.C.

Color: Olive grey above, whitish below.

Range: All oceans.

● SPINY DOGFISH   *Squalus acanthias*

The Spiny Dogfish is one of the few sharks whose age can be determined. This is done by counting the alternating light and dark bands on the second dorsal spine. Each dark band represents one winter's growth. These sharks are known to live up to 30 years.

Identifying Characteristics: No anal fin. Dorsal spines are mildly poisonous, and have been known to put an unwary fisherman in bed for a day. Pelvic fins are located approximately midway and opposite dorsal fins.

Size: Largest caught on U.S. coasts 5 ft. 3 in., but the average Spiny Dogfish closer to 3½ ft. in length.

Color: Slate-colored above. Pale grey to white below. Young often with white spots.

Range: Worldwide in temperate to subarctic waters. Found from shallows to 600 ft.

Blainville's Shark

● **BLAINVILLE'S SHARK**   *Squalus blainvillei*

The dorsal spines and lack of anal fin put this shark in the Dogfish family, but at present its exact classification is uncertain. It appears that several dogfish sharks of different scientific names may all be *Squalus blainvillei*.

Identifying Characteristics: Origin of first dorsal usually behind inner rear corner of pectoral fins. Body never marked with white spots; tail fin without notch near upper tip.

Size: Largest about 4 ft.

Color: Grey or brown, occasionally with darker markings.

Range: Hawaiian Islands and islands offshore Chili.

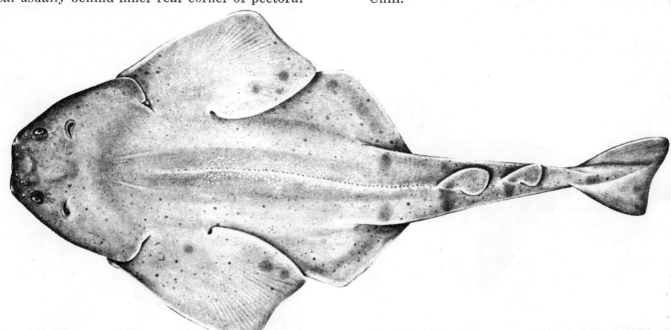

● **NORTHERN ANGEL SHARK**
    Squatina californica

The Angel Sharks are easy to differentiate from the rest of the sharks; they have a distinctly ray-like appearance, and lack totally the anal fin. Look closely, however, and you'll be able to tell the angel sharks from the rays; the pectoral fins of the angel sharks attach to the body, and not the head.

Identifying Characteristics: Body flattened; no anal fin; dorsals small and located far back on body.

Size: A little less than 5 ft.

Color: Dark brown.

Range: Gulf of California to southern Alaska.

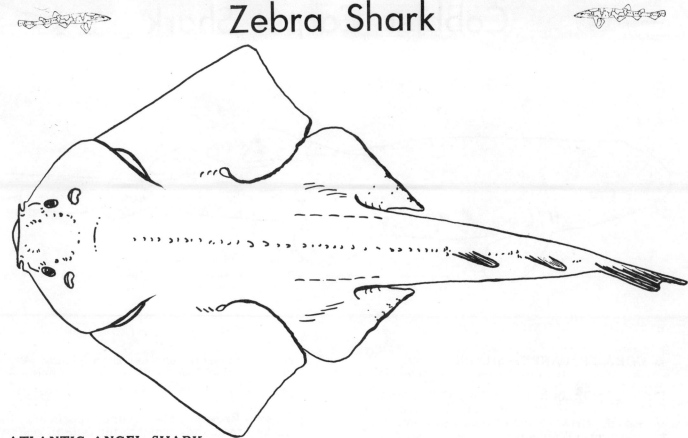

● ATLANTIC ANGEL SHARK
Squatina dumerili

Angel Sharks are more closely related to the rays than are the Saw Sharks; yet they are true sharks. For the most part, they are harmless, sluggish sharks.

Identifying Characteristics: Longer and wider than Northern Angel Shark; upper lobe of tail shorter than lower lobe.

Size: 4 to 5 ft.

Color: Upper surface grey or brown, with yellow to black tints. Usually blotched. Lower surface white.

Range: Southern New England to the northern Gulf of Mexico.

● ZEBRA SHARK   *Stegostoma fasciatum*

Also called Monkey-mouth Shark (India).

This is yet another brightly-patterned member of the nurse shark family. It is rather unusual, however, in the extremely long caudal fin. The tail is just about half the total length of the shark. Sluggish and harmless to man.

Identifying Characteristics: Very long tail. Snout short and blunt. Second dorsal very small. Pattern tends to fade somewhat with age.

Size: To 11 ft.

Color: Grey-brown with white or cream cross-bars.

Range: Entire Indo-Pacific area.

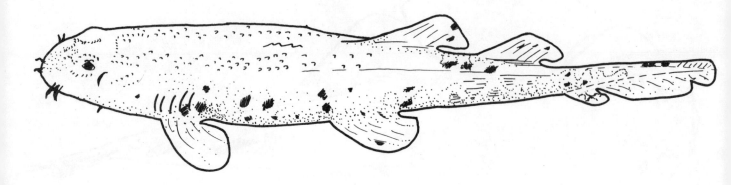

● COBBLER CARPET SHARK
Sutorectus tentaculatus

Paterned with an intricate design of tubercules on its back, the Cobbler Carpet Shark completes the circle around Australia started by the Northern Wobbeging.

Identifying Characteristics: Numerous, thin nasal barbles; spiracles larger than eyes; eyes set more closely together than in most Wobbegong sharks; back with rows of tubercules.

Size: 3 ft.

Color: Brown. The young specimens have dusky crossbands which later fade to scattered black spots. Lower surface yellow.

Range: South and West Australia.

● REEF WHITETIP SHARK
Triaenodon obesus

This is yet another shark with white-tipped fins. It differs from the Oceanic Whitetip in several characteristics, however, the major difference being the longer, more slender body.

Identifying Charactristics: Dorsal and tail fins tipped with white; flattened head; distinct nasal flaps. Teeth have several cusps, with the center cusp being the largest.

Size: Unusually large specimens may reach 7 ft.; more commonly about 5 ft.

Color: Dark to medium grey-brown; fins white tipped.

Range: Tropical Pacific, especially around islands. Only one specimen has been captured near the continental shelf.

Spotted Cat Shark

● **FEHLMANN SHARK**   *Tiakis fehlmanni*

The Fehlmann Shark is similar in body form, fin shape and fin position to the Dogfish. It differs, though, in head shape and the positioning of the gill rakers. Like so many of the rarer sharks, it probably feeds on small invertebrates such as shrimp.

Identifying Characteristics: Gill-rakers present, serving as feeding mechanism. Distinctive coloration pattern; back edges of nasal flaps scalloped; short labial furrows. Eyes large, and twice longer than high.

Size: Sexually mature at 18 in., the single length recorded for this shark.

Color: Basic color light tan, with a series of rich brown saddles on back spaced by smaller brown bars or spots. Lower surfaces yellowish white. Specimen was preserved in formalin, so the actual color pattern in life may not be as pronounced.

Range: The single specimen known was collected off the coast of Somalia in 1964.

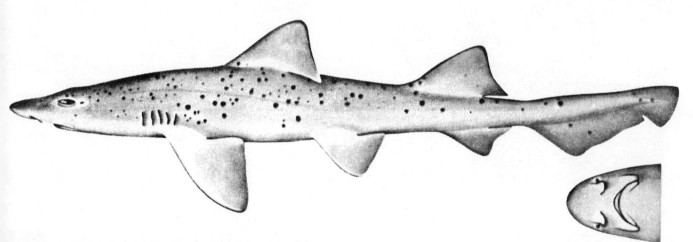

● **SPOTTED CAT SHARK**   *Triakis maculata*

Usually spotted but sometimes grey, the Spotted Cat Shark is known from the Peru-Chili area. A heavy-bodied shark, it has a short tail.

Identifying Characteristics: Head depressed. Small eyes; anal fin much smaller than second dorsal; tail short, less than ¼ total body length.

Size: To slightly less than 6 ft.

Color: Brownish-grey, with black spots. Edges of first dorsal usually black.

Range: Chili and Peru, usually in waters close to shore.

● **LEOPARD SHARK**   *Triakis semifasciata*

A grey or tan body with darker bars and stripes identify this recent addition to the family Carcharhinidae. Despite its name, the Leopard Shark is not nearly as aggressive as some other sharks; a single attack has been recorded.

Identifying Characteristics: Numerous dark bars and large dark spots on body; snout rather blunt; teeth usually with secondary cusps.

Size: Males grow to 5 ft.; females to 5½ ft.

Color: Tan to grey with darker blotches.

Range: Common in shallow waters of the Eastern Pacific. Usually found from Oregon to Baja California.

Small fish often benefit when a shark feeds nearby. Darting in, they pick up stray bits of food too small for the shark to eat. Some fish have found this arrangement works out well enough to warrant staying with the shark full-time. Three in particular are the Pilotfish, Remoras, and Sharksuckers. Because of this relationship, they are called *commensals*.

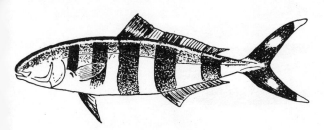

The Pilotfish (Naucrates ductor)

The Pilotfish is usually found swimming close to the dorsal fin of the shark, although it may venture out for short forays on its own. Its plump body has from 5 to 7 black vertical stripes on a bluish background. It averages 12 inches, in length, with occasional specimens up to 24 inches.

The scientific name of the Pilotfish, *Naucrates ductor,* is an amalgamation of Greek and Latin terms meaning "ruler of ships" and "leader". Despite these names, the Pilotfish neither leads nor pilots. It just follows. The names may re-

fer to the tendency of the fish to escort any large object. It may be a school of tuna, a turtle, a large boat, or even a large manta ray. Sharks are high on the preferred list, for several reasons.

First of these reasons is food. There may also be some protection in swimming close to a large shark. A moving shark also creates a bow pressure wave that can be ridden on, much like surface waves and surf-boards. Yet all these benefits provided by the shark do not gender loyalty. Pilotfish will leave a nonfeeding shark as soon as they spy one that is.

Remoras and Sharksuckers are closely related fish, belonging to the same family and grouped together under the common name "remoras". The family name of these fish is Echeinidae, meaning literally "those who hold back ships". Long ago it was a common belief that these fish could immobilize ships merely by clinging to them. Sharks and turtles were not affected by the clinging fish—just man-made conveyances.

Both the Remora and the Sharksucker can easily be recognized by the sucker disk on top of the head. This disk is actually a modified first dorsal fin. The strength of the suction is amazing, as anyone who has ever attempted to remove such a fish will agree. Pulling backwards only strengthens the suction. The fish must be slid to the side or forwards to be removed.

Dictionary of Sharks

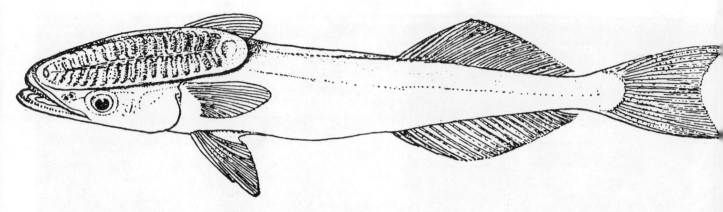

The Remora (Remora remora): a deep grey with no stripe.

The species most frequently found on sharks, *Remora remora*, is a deep sooty grey all over. It averages 2 feet in length, and is common in all temperate seas of the world. It may also be found in cooler waters, depending on where its chauffeur takes it. The adults can detach and swim to warmer waters, but the younger specimens evidently need the flow of water provided by the shark to get enough oxygen.

The Sharksucker, *Echeneis naucrates*, has a thinner body than the Remora and has a white-bordered dark stripe extending on each side from the snout to the tail. For the most part,

they are slightly shorter than the Remoras, usually reaching lengths of 12 inches. The record Sharksucker on file at Great Outdoors measured 35 inches and weighed 35 pounds 10 ounces. It was caught by Wayne Roper of Milwaukee, Wisc., March 23, 1968, while fishing with Capt. Jerry Hafly of the Yacht LEILANA, Nassau, Bahamas.

Sharks don't benefit from their relationship with Pilotfish. They do benefit slightly from the remoras, however. Remoras pay for the ride by consuming tiny shrimp-like parasites on the shark's skin.

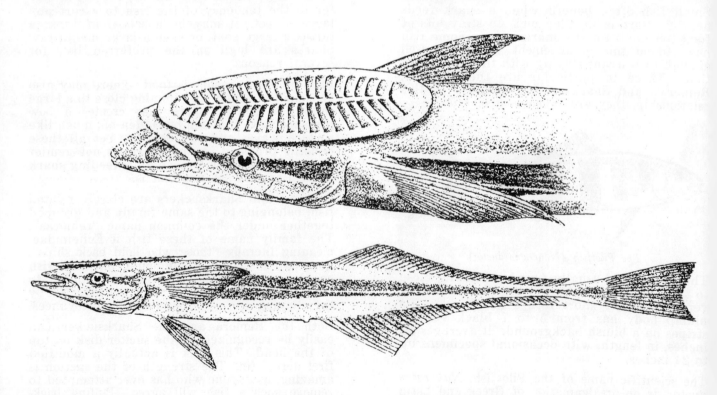

The Shark-sucker (Echeneis naucrates): black-and white striped

This chapter was written with the help of Bob Hughes, member of the Venice Shark Club in Florida. Bob began catching sharks in 1958, and since then has caught over 5200. Over 1500 of these have been caught on rod and reel. Photographs in this chapter are by Bob except as otherwise noted.

Man has fished shark for centuries. During WWII, sharks were harvested for their livers (rich in vitamin A), and for their durable hides. The picture has changed somewhat, but shark fishing can still be profitable. Prices given here are for the southeastern U.S. in 1973. Your area may vary.

The most valuable part of the shark is the skin. Properly scraped, salted and dried, a shark hide 60 inches long is worth $5.25 to $6.00. Tiger Shark hides are worth 50% more; Hammerheads, 50% less. Value of the hide decreases if it is scarred or blemished. The Ocean Hide and Leather Corporation in New Jersey is the principle U.S.-based company for these hides. They remove the denticles and tan the hide to produce a durable, handsome leather.

Shark fins, soaked in brine for a couple of days and then dried, bring from $1 to $3 a pound in Oriental markets. Boiled out, the cartilage yields a flavorless body to soups. Only the pectoral and first dorsal fins are used.

Shark flesh can bring the fisherman from twenty cents to thirty cents a pound when sent to Mexico and South American countries. It must be salted

Left: Bob Hughes displaying the teeth of a fresh-caught Dusky Shark. Hooked off Midnight Pass, Florida, the shark was about ¼ mile offshore, and in 10 to 15 feet of water. A small boat carried the bait out. Equipment here includes a shoulder harness, socket with polyfoam cushion, 13-foot Fenwick blank hollow glass rod with roller guides, cork handle, and heavy-duty seat.

and dried before shipment. If you'd like to avoid the bother of preparing the meat, you can sell it in coastal states for use as crab bait. Simply cut in hunks and with the skin left on, it makes sturdy bait for crab traps. It's worth about five cents to twelve cents a pound to the fisherman.

Shark meat can also be used for pet food, at eight cents to fifteen cents a pound. The remainder of the shark can be ground and used for fertilizer or for cattle feed. Used for fertilizer, it brings the fisherman ten to twenty cents a pound; the cattle-feed route is less profitable, at five to eight cents a pound. Shark meal makes excellent cattle feed; protein content is 8%.

Shark jaws can be cut out, cleaned and dried for ready sale to the novelty market. The amount they bring depends on size; small jaws, five inches in diameter, are worth $5. The larger jaws are worth more; a set twenty inches in diameter brings $50 to $100.

Even the shark eyes find a market. After boiling for an hour or so (preferably outdoors), they can be cut open and the hard, round lens removed. The lens can be drilled and strung for jewelery after drying. These "shark pearls" sell well in most tourist beach resorts.

Another novelty item uses the cartilagenous backbone. Cleaned, dried, strung on a metal rod and then varnished, it makes an unusual walking cane. Such canes are real conversation stoppers, and bring $50 to the maker.

Only recently, however, has the shark come into its own as a game fish. At this time, the International Game Fish Association recognizes six sharks as being true game fish. They are the White, Tiger, Mako, Blue, Porbeagle, and Thresher sharks. These sharks are found in both oceans, so any fisherman can take a go at hooking and landing one of these fighters.

Sharks can be fished day and night, and it isn't necessary to rent or own a boat to go after them. They can be fished from piers or bridges. If you do have access to a boat, however, and want to try the open waters, use a little common sense. Make sure your boat is large enough to provide some stability in the open waters. This means a length of no less than 15 feet, and broad enough beam to avoid tipping. The boat should also have enough freeboard to resist being swamped by a shark. Try fishing both still and adrift.

The pole is one of your first considerations. Length depends on whether you're pier or boat fishing. In pier fishing, a shorter, stouter pole

will give you more control over the shark. A length of 8 feet gives the best combination of strength and maneuverability.

In contrast, boat fishing gives you more room. If the shark makes a long run, you can start your engine and follow him. A longer pole can be used here. This longer pole will actually make playing the shark easier; the extra pole length is flexible, and takes up some of the shock of the shark's pulling.

One of the Calcutta solid bamboo poles will do well for shark fishing. The pole will bend while you're fishing, though, and when you're done will seem to have a permanent curve. Just hang the pole by its tip and weight the handle. An empty gallon milk jug, filled with water and tied to the rod butt, will provide enough weight.

If you want to be a little more elaborate, go for a solid fiberglass rod. Do avoid the hollow fiberglass rods; they may be less expensive, but they've been known to break when you hook a good-sized shark with some fight in him. Use a solid fiberglass rod in an 8 to 10-ft. length.

You may want to start with a blank solid fiberglass rod and put on the reel, guides and handle yourself. Cost for a rod this way—without the goodies you'll have to add on yourself—runs about $40 to 60. If you don't want to go with a blank rod, be sure the reel seat of the ready-made rod you buy is machined, and not stamped. The stamped seats tend to crack. Ready-made rods run from $40 to $100-plus.

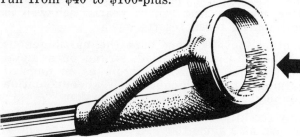

Rough, worn guides can fray your line.

The guides on your rod should be roller guides. The ordinary circular guides can become roughed by the constant line passage. These rough spots will wear your line and may break it. If you put your own guides on, wrap the pole first with EE thread. Put the guides on and wrap again to secure the guides. This double-under and double-over wrap holds the best. Coat with 2 coats color preserver and 4-8 coats of varnish.

The size of the reel you want on your rod will again depend on where you'll be fishing. Pier fishing requires a slightly larger reel—and a greater amount of heavier line—than does boat fishing. For instance, pier shark fishing might use a 12/0 to 16/0 reel with 900-1100 yards of 130-pound test line. Boat fishing could be accomplished using a 10/0 reel with 650 yards of 80-lb. test line. If you do go the boat route, remember

to use the harness lug on the top of the reel, or get a safety reel seat ring. Fasten the rod and reel to the boat via these rings so it can't be jerked overboard and lost.

The well-dressed shark fisherman. Note the shoulder harness and socket; padding on the socket would add comfort.

A socket or harness can be clipped on the reel to make it easier for you to deal with the shark's sudden pulls and turns. These are more effective than the auxiliary handle some anglers place above the reel. Cost for the harness will depend on the kind you get. A simple back harness— good for pier fishing—will run between $7 and $15. The kidney harness is slightly more, from $20 to $23. Sockets are about $7. You may well want to pad the back of the socket with a large hunk of foam. One of the new glues, labelled as effective on leather and foam rubber, will work to fasten the two together. Don't skimp on the foam, now. You will realize why the first time the butt end of a rod is hammered against your stomach for three hours straight. Try to find a hunk four inches thick, and as wide and as long as the leather base of the socket. The picture at the beginning of this section shows this well.

The handle of the rod is best covered with a material that will provide a good grip even when coated with water and fish slime. Either cork or rubber works well. Some anglers who start with a blank rod prefer a plastic-like putty they

mold to their grip before it hardens. Such a handle does provide a good grip, but if the pole should turn as the shark makes a sudden run to the right, your grip is broken at the precise moment a tight grip is vital.

Now that you've gotten your rod and reel, you need to think about what line to use. Generally, you won't want to use anything under 80-pound test. Line of this weight can land practically anything you can hook. But if you're going after the really big ones, use the 130-pound test. Other fishermen will smile at your naivite, but the smiles will stop when you pull in a 1000-pound Tiger.

For your terminal tackle, you can use either single-strand steel or braided leader wire. There are advantages to both. The single strand will fit between the teeth of the shark, and won't get cut in two. Unfortunately, it can kink and break. The braided wire is too thick to fit between the teeth and runs the risk of being chewed in two. The braided wire has the advantage in that it won't kink and break. A hundred yards of 80-pound test will cost about $3 to $3.50; the same amount of 130-pound test, $5.

The choice of leader is important when hunting sharks. Sharks, as you probably know, have extremely rough skin. A hooked shark often loops the leader around his body in an effort to get loose. The sharp edges of the fins and the rough skin cut ordinary line quickly. The wire leader keeps this from happening. Leader length can vary, but usually runs between 10 feet (boat fishing) and 20 feet (pier fishing—lots of sharp rocks and piles around). A good strong leader can be made from 1/16" stainless steel wire. Such a leader can take anything dished out. The wire is called "braided", but in actuality is only twisted.

You'll need special fasteners—called Nicopress fasteners—to crimp a sleeve against the doubled-back leader to fasten the leader to both the hook and the line. You can buy the crimping tool yourself for about $30. Sleeves are two for fifteen cents. Or you can take the line, leader and hook swivel to your local tackle dealer, and let him fasten it on. Incidentally, these fasteners are very strong and nigh-on to permanent. It takes a screwdriver, a vice, and a hammer to pry one off the leader. Unfortunately, the process shreds that section of leader beyond repair.

Next item on the rig is the hook. You want a forged hook, that is, one made out of a single piece of steel—not doubled back on itself and soldered—to withstand pulling. Size of the hook can vary, but 12-0 is a good intermediate size. Depending on the brand and the size of the hooks you choose, cost will run between forty and seventy cents a hook. These needle-eye hooks will rust out in the eye section if not taken care of properly but will not pull out as fast as regular hooks—even the welded hooks.

The most important prerequisites for bait is that it be oily and bloody. The oilier and bloodier the bait, the more scent will diffuse into the water, and the farther away sharks will be able to scent it. In the southeastern United States, Mullet, Bonito, Yellowtail Jack, Stingray, Skate, and Sheepshead are considered good baits, with Bonito and Mullet leading the list. Cut the bait into 1- to 2-pound chunks to use. Some fishermen believe "the larger the bait the bigger the fish" but smaller bait can be swallowed quickly. A large bait may only be held in the mouth as the shark swims away. The bait is then jerked from the shark's mouth before the hook has been set.

Many anglers use the "Sneaky Pete" arrangement when fastening bait onto hooks. This set-up uses two hooks imbedded in a whole fish for maximum hooking. The leader is passed through the gill of the fish and out through the mouth opening. The first hook is imbedded in the heaviest part of the fish, below the first dorsal fin. The trail or trace hook is imbedded farther back, about on a level with the anal fin.

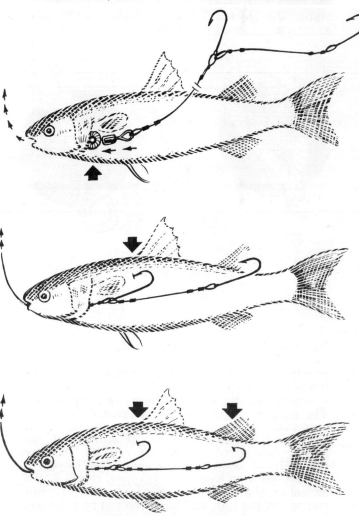

The Sneaky Pete rig.

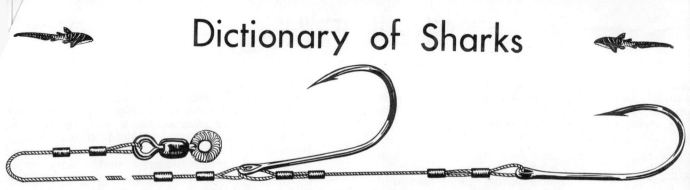

The entire Sneaky Pete rig, with wire leader attached.

Sometimes chumming is the only way you can draw sharks to your boat. Chumming consists of grinding up whole fish in a meat grinder, and letting driblets of the resultant mash fall into the water behind your boat to lay a scent trail. Some anglers consider chumming unsportsman-like. They put it on a par with spreading corn for deer, and then shooting the deer as they feed upon the corn. If you try chumming near shore, or worse yet, from a pier, you may find yourself in considerable trouble with the Coast Guard, police, and hoards of angry parents who insist you are drawing sharks to shore and increasing the chance of shark attacks. And they could be right. So, please, if you do chum, go well off-shore and don't do it any more than you have to.

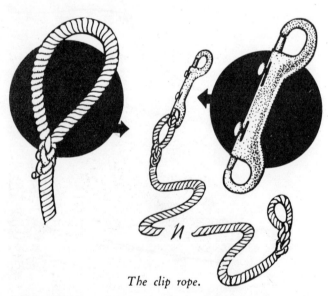

The clip rope.

One piece of equipment that could be considered more or less optional at this point is the snap or clip rope. This is essentially just as the name implies—a stout nylon (⅜" or ½") rope with a loop at one end and a harness clip at the other. The purpose of this rope is apparent if you've ever hauled a strong fish close to your boat and then tried to hold him there. A strong fish, no matter how tired he is, can call up uncanny reservoirs of strength. The snap rope, looped to a cleat on the boat and snapped through the swivel on the line end of the leader, will permit you to cut the line, and hand the rod to someone. You can then concentrate on getting the shark subdued. Besides being stronger than the line,

it is much easier to grab and won't leave gouge furrows in your hands as the shark struggles. It is wise not to laugh too much at this point. One hundred-thirty pound test, looped around a finger and then jerked as the shark heads for the depths, can remove a finger pretty quickly.

If you like, a shock cord can be spliced into the clip rope. The shock cord is actually just a strip of strong rubber, and it cushions the line against the shark's thrashing.

A tired yet wary Tiger Shark being hauled up to the boat.

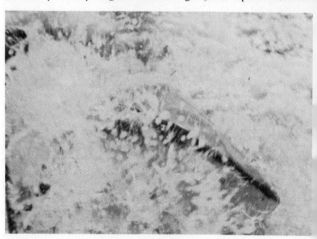

The same Tiger after deciding he doesn't like what he sees. This is why a clip rope is a good idea—such a shark has an incredible amount of pull.

Once the shark is hauled up to the boat, you'll need to gaff him if you're going to bring him on board. A flying gaff—essentially a long pole with a large fish-hook fastened on one end—is usually used when boat fishing. Hook the shark anywhere, but near the gills is best. The main disadvantage to a regular gaff is that a gaffed

shark can beat you to death with the gaff handle while you're trying to finish him off. When a flying gaff hooks the shark, the handle comes free. This leaves the hook in the shark and the line in your hands.

If you're pier fishing, a grappling hook—the kind used for scaling walls—can be used. This handy device has three or four hooks on it, as compared to the single hook on the regular gaff. Gaffing is easier when a four-hook gaff is used.

At this point, you may want to add a bangstick to your tackle. A bangstick, discussed more completely in the chapter on shark attack, is basically a metal tube with a shotgun shell and a firing pin in one end. When the bangstick is pushed against a shark's head, the shell is pushed against the firing pin. The shell is fired, and plunges directly into the shark's head. It is an effective and fast way to kill sharks.

Some anglers feel the bangstick is an unnecessary expense. Many is the fisherman who carries a stout baseball bat or sledgehammer to crack a hooked shark on the head. This is all well and good if done correctly, but smacking a struggling shark hard enough to kill him isn't easy. Rube Allyn, the founder of this publishing company, found this out the hard way when his helper missed the shark and stove in the stern planking of their boat, five miles offshore.

Once you've hooked a shark, how can you tell what kind it is or how big it is before you've pulled him in? Here in the southeastern United States, you have some hint as to the kind of the shark by where you hooked him. Lemon and Bull sharks are often hooked near beaches; Nurses near coral and rocks; Tigers in deeper water, and Hammerheads in open water. If it's Tarpon season, the Hammerheads come closer to shore to feed upon the Tarpon.

Behavior can also indicate what kind of shark you've hooked. The Nurse Shark fights some, and twists when near the boat. Hammerheads pull hard, and don't give up easily. Lemon Sharks are good for one 150-yard run. This behavior is true for the southeastern U.S. areas; it may well vary in other regions.

Even the season of the year can point to the kind of hooked shark. Around Sarasota, Florida, October through April means Brown, Dusky, Bull and Tiger sharks are caught. The summer months—May through August—bring Lemon, Nurse, Bull, Tiger and Hammerhead sharks in. February is the month for Great White Sharks.

The behavior of a hooked shark even gives a clue to its size. Smaller sharks run fast without hesitation. The bigger sharks are more deliberate, and lack the quick reaction time of the smaller sharks. But even the most experienced shark fisherman can be fooled. Conditions under water may change, or perhaps several sharks are after the bait.

A few words of caution regarding hooked sharks. If at all possible, don't bring them into the boat at all; tie them alongside until you get back to port. There is only one way to remove the hook from a shark's mouth without being bitten. Wait until the next day. No matter how you prop or wedge the mouth open, the shark is all too likely to twist and nail you with his teeth. The only way you can avoid this is to wait until the shark is completely, unmistakably dead.

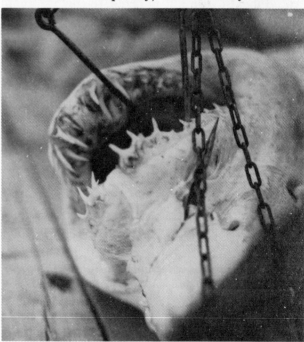

Teeth like the Sand Tiger's show why it is best to wait a day before trying to retrieve a hook. Not known to be dangerous in Florida, the Sand Tiger is considered a hazard in Australian waters.

A hooked Tiger unwittingly displays some key identification points—blunt, squared-off nose; nostrils deeply indented, and teeth notched on outer edge. This particular shark was caught on a set line off Ft. Pierce, Florida.
Picture by John DeBry

Don't believe all those people who scoff at shark meat and claim the shark is a trash fish. It isn't true. Shark meat ranks alongside Swordfish in texture and flavor. Shark does, however, lack the high concentrations of mercury so frequently found in Swordfish.

Many countries are familiar with the good taste of shark. In Japan, the gelatinous fins are used in making Shark Fin Soup, and the meat as a main dish. Filets of young sharks comprise one of the most popular dishes in Yucatan. Britons have been relishing the ubiquitous "fish and chips" for years. Yet the "fish" is frequently shark, rather than a true bony fish. In America, the fine white fish filets in grocery store freezer cases so cheerfully labelled "Swordfish" or "Cod" may sometimes more accurately be termed "Shark."

There are six kinds of sharks considered best for eating. These are the Great White Shark, Mako, Porbeagle, Thresher (both kinds), and Dogfish. Two others, the Small Dusky and the Hammerheads, follow closely on this list. Unfortunately, the flesh of the huge Basking Shark is too flabby for use as food.

To avoid the ammonia taste characteristic of poorly-prepared shark, prepare and ice the meat as soon as possible. Clean the shark much as you would any other fish. Remove the skin and the underlying layer of dark meat, and cut the shark into filets. Soak the refrigerated meat overnight in brine, to further avoid ammonia flavor.

SMOKING

Either a homemade or commercially-constructed smoker works well for shark. Heat up the smoker and place the rinsed filets in the drawer. Sprinkle well with salt. Close the smoker and let it smoke for an hour. Baste with melted butter or margarine. If by any chance you skipped soaking the meat in brine, resalt after every basting.

Repeat the basting at 3-hour intervals until the fish is done and turns golden. Total smoking time for steaks an inch to an inch-and-a-half thick will be about 6 to 8 hours at 115°. Up to 25 or 30 hours will be needed for cold-smoked shark.

For further instructions on smoking sea-food, see "How To Smoke Seafood" by Ted Dahlem, $1.00, Great Outdoors Publishing Company.

COOKING

If you don't want to wait 25-30 hours for your shark, it can be prepared much as any other fish. Fry, bake, or broil it—any good fish recipe will compliment the flavor of this fish. Use your favorite recipe or one of those below. The recipes here are tried-and-true shark recipes, with the ingredients and cooking times adjusted accordingly.

SHARK, OVEN-FRIED

2 pounds fresh shark filets
½ cup rich milk
1 cup dry bread crumbs
⅛ teaspoon basil
⅓ cup melted butter or margarine
1½ teaspoon salt
dash pepper
2 tablespoons chopped parsley

Wipe filets with damp cloth. Pour milk into small mixing bowl. Add salt, pepper and basil. Stir well. Dip each filet in seasoned milk then in bread crumbs. Arrange in buttered shallow baking dish and pour melted butter on fish. Bake at 350 to 375 degrees 30 minutes. Serves 6.

 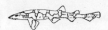
SHARK MARSEILLAISE

2 pounds fresh Sand Shark filets
1 onion, minced
1 tablespoon chopped parsley
1 clove garlic, minced
½ cup dry Sauterne wine
3 firm tomatoes, diced
3 tablespoons cooking oil
  salt and pepper

Wipe filets with damp cloth. Pour oil in oven-proof dish, place over medium flame. Add onion, parsley, garlic, tomatoes, salt and pepper to taste. Place filets carefully over top of vegetables. Cover and bring to boil. Lower flame. Simmer for 15 minutes. Add wine and bring to boil. Transfer dish to 350 degree oven. Bake 10 minutes or until fish flakes easily with fork. Carefully remove fish from sauce using large spatula. Arrange filets on preheated platter. Keep warm. Strain sauce through fine sieve and heat to boiling. Sauce should be reduced by this time. Pour hot sauce over filets and serve.

BLUE FIN LATINO

3 pounds shark filets
  oil
3 medium onions, sliced thin
1 1-pound 14-ounce can tomatoes
1 sweet red pepper sliced thin or
    minced
2 tablespoon oil
2 tablespoon lemon juice
1 tablespoon chili powder

Sear fish on both sides in hot oil. Remove to a well oiled baking pan. Spread thin slices of onion on fish and pour canned tomatoes over top. Mix red pepper, oil, lemon juice and chili powder and sprinkle over top of fish. Bake at 350 deg. 30 min. Makes 8 servings.

BLUE FIN MELANGE

2 tablespoons butter or margarine
2 tablespoons flour
1 cup milk
½ cup heavy cream
3 cups flaked cooked shark filets
½ teaspoon chili powder
⅛ teaspoon cayenne
  salt, pepper
  toasted tortilla chips

Melt butter and blend in flour. Gradually add milk and cream and cook and stir until thickened. Add sauce to shark meat. Season with chili powder, cayenne and salt and pepper to taste. Heat over low heat. Serve with toasted tortilla chips. Makes 4 servings.

POACHED SHARK REMOULADE

  shark filets
  sliced onion, optional
  water
2 tablespoons lemon juice
2 tablespoons tarragon vinegar
2 tablespoons prepared mustard
2 tablespoons horseradish
1 tablespoon parsley
1 teaspoon paprika
¼ teaspoon cayenne
1 cup oil
¼ cup finely chopped celery
¼ cup finely chopped green onion
1 tablespoon minced capers

Place shark filets in deep baking pan. Top with onion slices, if desired. Add water until pan is half full. Bake at 400 deg. 45 min. Serve with Remoulade Sauce. To make Sauce, mix lemon juice, vinegar, mustard, horseradish, parsley, paprika and cayenne. Beat in oil, then add celery, green onion and capers.

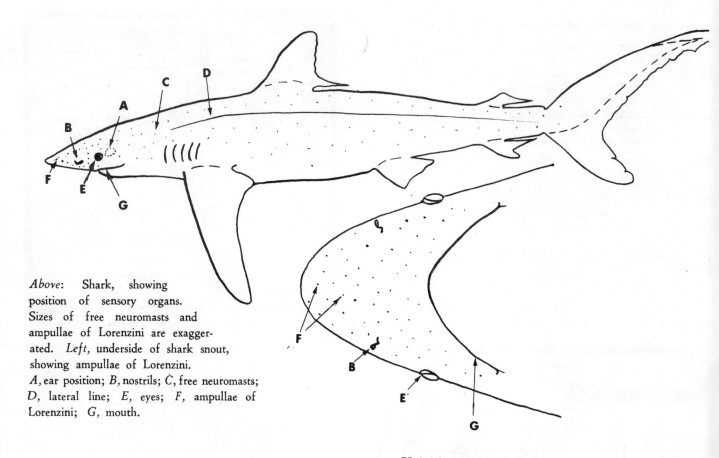

Above: Shark, showing position of sensory organs. Sizes of free neuromasts and ampullae of Lorenzini are exaggerated. *Left,* underside of shark snout, showing ampullae of Lorenzini.
A, ear position; *B,* nostrils; *C,* free neuromasts; *D,* lateral line; *E,* eyes; *F,* ampullae of Lorenzini; *G,* mouth.

Sharks are extremely efficient when it comes to finding food. They employ several senses, each most effective within a set distance from the food. The closer the shark is to the food, the more senses come into play, telling the shark where—and what—the food is.

Perhaps the longest-range device is hearing. Sharks are attracted to low-frequency pulsed sounds, and they are able to detect these sounds from distances measuring in the thousands of yards.

Olfaction comes into play next, at a range of about 500 yards. The nostrils of the shark don't open directly into the mouth as they do in frogs. Instead, they are baffled so swimming creates a constant water flow over sensory cells within the nasal cavity. The shark turns to whatever side has the stronger impulse. As long as the shark swims, he has constant tabs on the odors around him. It's an automatic process and requires no effort on the shark's part. The sensitivity of this organ is impressive. Sharks can sense one part mammal blood to 10 or even 100 million parts water.

Yet blood is not the only odor that interests a shark. Scared fish give off an odor or secretion that provokes hunting activity in sharks. Albert Tester of the University of Hawaii found this out in a series of experiments conducted in 1960. His method was basically as follows:

Put some uninjured fish in 2 containers of sea water. Label one container "A" and put it aside in some quiet place. Label the other container "B" and do your best to scare the fish to death. Yell at them. Beat on the sides of the container with a big stick or frypan and spatula.

Now siphon some of the water from container "A" into a shark pen. The sharks will respond to the siphoned water with mild hunting activity which will soon stop.

Siphon some of the water from container "B" into the shark pen. Tester found that strong hunting activity resulted, with some of the circling sharks even biting the end of the siphon tube.

As the shark gets closer to the food, the lateral line begins detecting. It functions as a displacement detector. This means that the line can sense movement in the water; struggling fish will create tiny ripples or currents in the water (no matter what the depth) which stimulate the lateral line.

Now that the shark is closer to the food, consider the pit organs. Pit organs, or free neuromasts, are sensory cells scattered all over the surface of the shark. Whereas the sensory cells of the lateral line respond to the light touch of water displacement, free neuromasts respond to changes in salinity—no matter what causes this change. A heavy rainfall will often result in an accumulation of sharks near the shore. They're probably feeding on animal debris washed down rivers. The neuromasts are used to detect this change, and the shark homes in on the stimulus. Pit organs are effective for ranges of several hundred yards.

At a distance of about 50 feet, eyesight comes into play. The eyes of all sharks are loaded with rods, the nerve cells sensitive to light and dark on a black-and-white basis only. Because of these, a shark can easily differentiate between an object and its background. This differentiation is particularly enhanced if the object is moving; then the displacement-sensitive lateral line can also detect the object. So now the shark can see what it's been homing in on. But that's not enough. There's one more sense.

Look at the nose of the next shark you see. Those little taste-bud appearing dots on the nose are called the ampullae of Lorenzini. They are sensitive to temperature (and therefore can detect warming or cooling water) as well as touch. Some experiments conducted by A. J. Kalmijn indicate that at short distances the ampullae are also sensitive to the electric potentials of fish. Short distances here mean anything from a few inches to actual contact. In fact, the nudge sometimes given potential food before the actual strike may be for the purpose of verifying identification.

Sometimes a shark seems to skip some of these sensory stages. If an object checks out all right on the first few steps, the shark can often skip the remainder and swallow the food before anything else does. Unfortunately, this doesn't always work out. Sharks have been found with an amazing variety of items in their stomachs, ranging from soft drink bottles to rolls of tar paper. Yet this doesn't present a real problem. When the stomach of the shark becomes too full with these junk items, it merely regurgitates the whole mess and starts over.

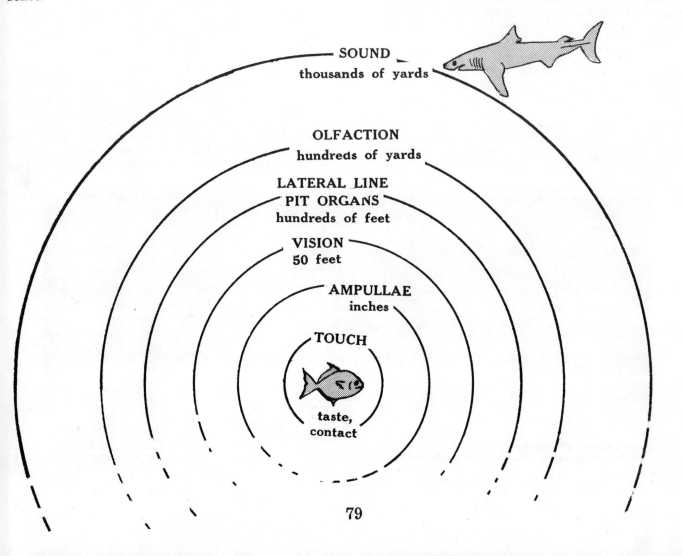

SOUND
thousands of yards

OLFACTION
hundreds of yards

LATERAL LINE
PIT ORGANS
hundreds of feet

VISION
50 feet

AMPULLAE
inches

TOUCH

taste, contact

As far back as man has walked erect, and certainly in recorded time, he has been the victim of shark attacks. One of the earliest recorded shark attacks was depicted on a vase excavated from Ischia, Italy, an island just west of what is presently Napoli. The vase pictures a man being eaten by a shark-like fish and has been dated 725 BC. Later historic references include the records of Antonio Pigafetta, who sailed with Vasco de Gama. Pigafetta described the "teeth of a terrible kind" and the man-eating tendencies of sharks. Olaus Magnus of Sweden printed a shark-attack picture in the mid-1500's.

As might be expected from the law of averages alone, the United States has had its share of shark attacks. One black two-week period in 1916 saw five attacks along the coast of New Jersey. But it wasn't until 1959 that a systematic study of shark attacks began.

In 1959, the Shark Research Panel of the American Institute of Biological Sciences began the Shark Attack File. Similar panels were begun in Australia and South Africa. These research panels began gathering first-hand accounts, witnesses' reports, and newspaper clippings of shark attacks. Analysis of the accumulated information in the United State's File was turned over to Dr. Dave Baldridge.

Reports began arriving from all over the world. The more information the Panel gathered, the harder it became to establish a set attack behavior or find factors common to the majority of cases. Even the identity of the attacking shark was hard to establish. Less than 5% of all shark attacks identified to shark positively. This means that all the "Dangerous Shark" lists were drawn from a sample that amounted

Known Attackers	
Great White Shark	Bull
Hammerheads	Blue
Mako	Lemon
Tiger	Grey Nurse

One listing of dangerous shark species. This is not a complete list; such a list would be much longer. This is just a basic list of sharks known to be hazardous.

to less than 5% of the whole! Of course, these lists were and are still a good basic guide of what kinds to avoid. But there may well be some species not listed as dangerous simply because they haven't been identified as such.

Information gathered by the File began to indicate fallacies in the classic shark attack theories. Some of these theories were correct, but for the wrong reasons. For instance, most shark atacks occur within 150 yards of the shore. But it isn't that sharks won't grab someone 151 yards out: it's just that few people go further out than 150 yards. Water depth may be a factor, here. Only a third of shark attacks occur in water deeper than 5 feet.

Still other theories stated that sharks wouldn't attack in water colder than 70 degrees F. This could be for two reasons; one, almost no one will go into water colder than 70 degrees—it's just too cold. Secondly, the shark (being a cold-blooded beast) slows down when the water is cold. He doesn't use as much energy, and doesn't require as much food. These two

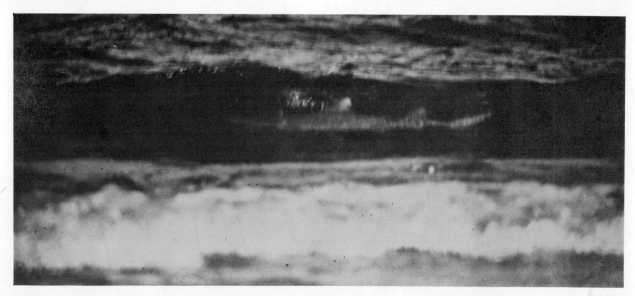

Lemon Shark feeding in a breaker, just offshore. Three to four sharks were visible in each breaker.   Photo by Bob Hughes.

factors help explain the so-called "shark-attack seasons". These seasons range from May to October in the Northern Hemisphere (42 degrees N to 21 degrees N latitude), and from November to April in the Southern Hemisphere (42 degrees S to 21 degrees S). These "seasons" correspond to the spring and summer seasons in each hemisphere; the times when the most people are in the water. Near the equator—where it's always warm—attacks occur all year around.

As time went on, more weak spots in the older shark attack theories appeared. If attack sites are dotted on a world map, the waters of Sydney, Australia, and the Tampa Bay area, Florida, are almost solidly dotted. This doesn't mean that hungry sharks prowl these waters and grab anyone in them; it's just that the high populations mean more swimmers.

Another theory stated swimming after 1 PM to be dangerous, and cited figures that showed most attacks occurred in the afternoon. But if the number of people in the water is plotted against the time of day, it turns out that more people swim after noon than in the morning.

NIGHT SWIMMING CAN BE RISKY

As evening falls, the "1 PM theory" becomes correct. Statistics show that 5.4% of shark attacks occur after 7 PM. The percent of night swimmers is considerably less than 5.4%. Swimming in the dark is unmistakably riskier than day swimming. This is logical, though— some fish are night feeders, and if a shark is hungry he'll be looking for these fish. Reduced vision means the shark may grab anything that look interesting.

Dr. Baldridge noted the population size-shark attack parallel, and began to run checks. Data he has gathered indicates a direct relationship between the number of swimmers and the number of attacks in that area. Broadly speaking, it isn't so much a matter of water depth, temperature, season, or geographical location; the prime factor is people in the water. It's that simple.

As crosschecks were run on the reported attacks, common factors began to appear. Naturally, not all factors were present in all attacks. Sharks are a lot like hurricanes in that both are inconsistant and unpredictable. But there appear to be certain factors that will affect a shark's behavior.

For instance, wearing a boldly striped or patterned swimming suit may be hazardous. Sharks deal in black and white because they can't see colors. They only see shades of gray. An object that offers strong black-and-white value contrast—be it stripes or whatever—will attract a shark's attention. He may not be hungry. But he's watching . . .

STRONG CONTRAST ATTRACTS SHARKS

Black wet-suits used to be considered about the safest garb. Unfortunately, you have to watch your diving location. Off the coast of California, sharks eat sea lions. And evidence indicates sharks have trouble discriminating between sea lions and black wet-suit-clad divers.

Secondly, it is unwise to tie a string of bleeding fish to your belt when spear fishing. A shark may be interested only in fish, but he won't be picky. If you're in the way when he goes for the fish, you'll get nailed. If a shark looks interested in your fish, don't waste time arguing. Also don't go in the water when you're bleeding.

If a shark comes this close, he may be just looking. In case he isn't, though, back off calmly.

NEVER, EVER ARGUE WITH SHARKS.

Occasionally a shark will break away from the normal shark population and stay near one particular stretch of coast. This can be for several reasons. Perhaps the shark is old or crippled, and can no longer compete actively for food. He could be just lazy. So he hangs around the shore, and eats what he happens across. This could be offal from a fishing pier, debris from a river, or garbage in a large harbor. As time goes on, the shark learns the territory and becomes bolder. The coastline he "patrols" becomes hazardous for people, simply because sharks are unpredictable. The shark has become a member of what is termed the *accesory population*, an adjunct to the normal shark population. Call him a rogue, a stray, a bank-loafer, or whatever, but watch out for him.

Sharks are attracted to an area by recent heavy rains. The reason for this is pretty logical; rain washes dead animals down streams, and this makes for pretty good shark food. The sharks respond both to the scent of dead animals and to the decreased salinity caused by the increased stream flow. Swimming in these waters may be risky, especially if the water is murky. The murkiness will obscure the shark's vision; excited by the scent of food, he is likely to grab anything that attracts his attention.

In trying to establish these attack trends, Dr. Baldridge found that not all sharks seemed to be attacking because of hunger. In fact, the sharks weren't really biting at all; the wounds they left seemed to be more scratch marks from the teeth instead of true bites. (Bear in mind here, though, that what may be scratches to a shark may be long, deep lacerations to a human being.) And yet these "scratches" were not the result of poor aim on the shark's part. The shark appeared to be saying simply "Buzz off." A brief look at the shark's nose will help explain this behavior.

As described in the chapter on "How a Shark Finds Its Food", sharks often nudge their prey before biting. This nudge brings little taste-bud-appearing nodules on the underside of the shark's nose into contact with the prey. These buds, the ampullae of Lorenzini, are sensitive to touch, temperature, and electric potential. They are one of the final ways a shark identifies his food. If a shark opens his mouth slightly before nudging, the snout can be elevated more, and the ampullae get better contact with the object. If the object turns out to be worth eating, well, the teeth and mouth are right there and ready for action. But in any case the contact may push the teeth against the supposed "victim", scraping the skin. The released blood would further serve to identify the victim. Shark, uninterested, pulls his nose down and swims away. But the "victim" is left with the rake-marks of a shark's teeth on his leg or body. Has he really been the victim of a shark attack, or just the object of a shark's curiosity?

TERRITORIAL RIGHTS. UNDERWATER.

Dr. Baldridge points out that most animals have their own "turf"—an area that belongs to them and must be defended from intruders. Sharks may well have the same sense of territoriality. An intruder construed as a possible threat is subject to the same warning—a quick slash with the upper teeth. In meaning, the slash is the equivilant of a dog's growl. The area the shark is defending doesn't have to be 50 square yards of ocean floor; it could be the water surrounding the shark. Any intruder that gets too close may be warned.

But before you swear never to go swimming at a beach again, relax. Like everything else, being attacked by a shark is a matter of probabilities. You have a 1 in 5 million chance of being attacked by a shark. You stand a better chance of being struck by lightning next time you run out to close your car windows when it rains. And a much better chance of having your fender crunched at the next light. Take the precautions outlined in this chapter, and enjoy yourself!

No government stepped into the shark-attack picture until WWII. At that time, it became apparent that too many airmen and sailors were hitting the ocean and not coming out alive. As the result of these well-documented shark attacks on military men, the US Naval Research Laboratory embarked on an extensive yet often frustrating search for an effective shark repellent. Many compounds were tested, including some known poisons such as arsenic and cyanide. But the low metabolism of sharks proved to be a handicap in developing a repellent—sharks are rather primitive beasts, and it takes a lot of anything to kill them. Any poison you dump into the water may kill the person it is supposed to protect before the slowly-reacting shark knows that there is anything noxious there.

Shark Chaser can be used on fishermen's lines to protect a hooked fish from attack.

Securely pinned to thousands of life jackets, Shark Chaser helped lessen the fear of shark attack for many military men during WWII.

Shark fishermen supplied the fact that sharks were repelled by decaying shark flesh. Using this information as a base, the Research Laboratory developed a repellent they called Shark Chaser. A mixture of ammonium acetate, copper acetate, and nigrosin dye, the repellent combined two theories into one small, 6½-ounce package. The first two ingredients were actually to repel the sharks. The nigrosin dye formed a dark cloud in the water, much like the camoflaging clouds emitted by squid. Both repelled by the chemical odor in the water, and unable to tell if there was anything to eat in the dark dye cloud, sharks would theoretically give up and swim off. The chaser lasted from two to four hours in the water.

As time went on, it became obvious that Shark Chaser was not the final answer. Although some seemed repelled by it, other sharks ignored it. Further tests in various shark-infested waters of the globe (including Bimini, Ecuador, and a small atoll off the southwest coast of Mexico) indicated that the effectiveness of Shark Chaser

depended on several factors: the area in which the repellent was tested (sharks in some parts of the world just seem to be more aggressive than sharks in other parts of the world); the type of shark being tested (some sharks, such as the Whitetip or the Great White Shark are more aggressive than other species); and even the mood of the individual sharks. Sharks in a feeding frenzy paid no attention to the repellent, no matter where the tests took place.

Several other tacks were tried in the battle to discourage sharks. One of these, the bubble curtain, was designed for beach protection. It consisted mainly of a weighted air hose, punctured with a series of holes, connected to an air compressor. Bubbles drifting upwards supposedly presented an impenetrable barrier to sharks. At first, the curtain seemed to work. But the deterrent effect disappeared as sharks became accustomed to the curtain. A rigorous test by Perry Gilbert in 1961 dispelled any faint hopes that shark attacks at the beach were a thing of the past. Of 12 Tiger Sharks tested, the majority showed no hesitance at swimming through the curtain after an hour. After 26 hours of testing, only one of the sharks continued to avoid the curtain. From the statistician's viewpoint, the test was only 8.3% effective—and that wasn't good enough.

Another beach safeguard was the shark fence. This was a wire mesh fence covering the entire mouth of a cove or bay. No fish larger than the mesh could get through. Good in basic concept, this type of beach protection had two disadvantages. The initial cost for material and installation was high, especially if the mouth of the bay was wide. Beside the original cost, wave damage and corrosion meant frequent repairs.

Shark meshing was the logical progression from the shark fence. Meshing consisted of a series of gill nets, anchored offshore at staggered intervals. The nets caught sharks both coming and going. They were checked at intervals, and

any captured sharks removed. This method has proven to be valuable, despite high maintenance costs (the nets tear easily). The decrease in the number of shark attacks in areas where the beaches are meshed can probably be attributed to the decreased local shark population. Oddly enough, the meshing does not provide full-scale protection for the beach—there are gaps between the nets sharks could easily negotiate.

Protection for the individual has progressed further than beach protection. Here we must use a broader term than "repellent"; although the following methods employ several tactics, they all amount to the same thing—shark defense.

The bangstick delivers a lead slug directly to the shark's brain.

Offensive measures against sharks have made great strides in the last ten years. First on this list is the bangstick or powerhead. This is merely a length of steel tubing, with a chamber for a 12-gauge shotgun shell and a firing mechanism together at one end. This end of the cylinder is plugged with petroleum jelly to protect the shell and firing mechanism from salt water. If a shark gets too close (or if the hooked shark is drawn up to your boat), the powerhead is jammed between the shark's eyes. The thrust drives the

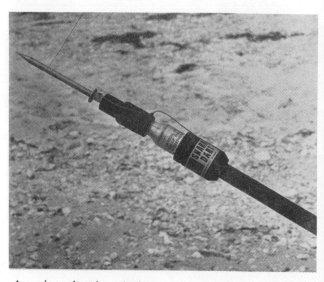

A carbon dioxide cylinder—the kind used to inflate life preservers—powers the carbon dioxide shark dart.

shell against the firing pin, and the shell detonates. The slug is propelled into the brain of the shark, killing him instantly. Because the charge goes directly into the shark, it is not slowed by water resistance. The concussion can jolt the diver, but that beats an actual shark attack, any day.

Two of the most recent shark defense methods for divers are based on detailed knowledge of shark physiology. For instance, the ability of the shark to swim depends on a delicate relationship among the lifting force of the fins (*i.e.,* fin size), the shark's weight, and the amount of oil in the shark's liver. These three factors are set for each species of shark—each species has a set fin size:weight:liver oil proportion that permits it to control the depth at which it swims. If this balance is altered, the shark can no longer control his depth in the water. This knowledge, coupled with a simple carbon dioxide cylinder, forms the basis for one of the most decisive shark deterrents. The carbon dioxide cartridge is fitted into a special steel holder tipped with a strong hollow needle. When the shark rushes the diver, the needle is plunged into the fleshy part of the shark's body. The force of the blow pushes a tiny needle into the stem end of the cartridge. The compressed carbon dioxide is injected directly into the shark's body. This added buoyancy propels the wriggling shark straight to the surface—and often kills him outright as well.

The second type of shark "needle" is an electric dart. Basically, the dart is a four-inch blade attached to a small (1¼ inch-square) battery. An electrode at the tip of the blade is connected to one battery terminal, and the other terminal is in contact with the water. The battery generates 30 volts—sufficient to paralyze a twelve-foot, 450-pound Tiger Shark. The dart is usually carried on the end of a ten-foot sea lance. When

the blade is thrust into a shark, the dart detaches from the lance. The electrodes complete an electric circuit between the dart, the shark, and the ocean. Depending on the size of the shark, it is either killed outright or paralyzed for the life of the battery (about ten minutes). This gives the diver ample time to get out of the area. As miniaturization improves, the longer-lived battery will increase paralysis time.

Another electronic defense—the Hick's repeller—is based on the fact that a specific electronic frequency will repell a specific species of shark. The larger the shark, the more effective the device. Originally designed as a hand-held device, looking rather like a set of TV rabbit ears, continued modifications will give us a repellent that will be built into a wetsuit.

If you don't want to go the offensive route, there are more methods open to you. One, coupled with the standard Shark Chaser, has proven especially useful to downed airmen. Called the Johnson Shark Bag after the inventor, the device is a large, black plastic bag with three inflatable rings at the top. The flier merely inflates the rings with air, tips the bag to fill it with water, and climbs in. The bag presents no attractive, bite-size projections, the way a floating man might; it seals in any inticing odors such as blood; and it helps conserve body heat. The dark color does not attract a shark's attention. The brightly colored rings at the top aid sighting by rescue craft. The whole thing folds up into an "easy-toting" size. The only real disadvantage to this method of defense is its extreme fraility. Once the bag has been torn, odors can escape. A shark close by would be quick to realize that bag was nothing more than a drab piñata.

The last shark deterrent is, to this time, the only 99.9% sure way of avoiding shark attack under any conditions—even during feeding frenzies. This is the shark cage, used by so many underwater photographers in obtaining close-up shots of sharks. Looking much like a human-sized bird cage, the shark cage is constructed from steel, with buoyancy controls. The bars of the cage are too close together to permit entrance by any but the smallest sharks. These were the cages used in filming the documentary, "Blue Water, White Death". Their effectiveness has been clearly demonstrated, although their mobility has not.

Filled with water and hanging upright in the water, the Johnson Shark Bag screens from the shark both the sight and smell of an injured person. Big enough for two in a squeeze, the bag provides considerable psychological comfort.

Information Please

Only about 120 different sharks are pictured and described in this book. Many sharks were left out for lack of information. A few of these are listed below. Some of the book's information may become outdated due to nomenclature changes, new research, or field observations. If you know of a species not included, a record size or different distribution for a shark already described, or have any other comments, please write the author at:

Great Outdoors Publishing Company
4747 28th St. North
St. Petersburg, Fla. 33714

Your field reports will be appreciated.

Information Solicited On These Species

Carcharhinus menisorrah (Grey Reef Shark)
Centroscyllium granulosum
Centroscymnus crepidator
Etmopterus hillianus
Etmopterus lucifer
Etmopterus unicolor
Etmopterus villosus
Isistius pludotus
Oxynotus bruniensis
Oxynotus caribbaeus

Oxynotus paradoxus (Spritsail Shark)
Paragaleus gruveli
Paragaleus pectoralis
Somniosus antarticus
Somniosus longus
Somniosus rostratus
Squaliolus laticaudus (Long-Faced Dwarf Shark)
Squaliolus sarmenti (Atlantic Dwarf Shark)
Sphyrna couardi
Triakis acutipinna

Index

Subject

More of Great Outdoors

Dictionary of Fishes — This is the most-used and largest-selling fish identification book ever published. Over 400,000 copies in use today. Includes world records; common names; habits and food value. Size 8½x11. Soft cover $1.95.

Skin and Scuba — Revised edition of this popular book. Packed with information on equipment, signals, spearfishing, photography, and the dangers and problems the diver might encounter. Size 8½x11. Soft cover $1.50.

How to Cook Your Catch by Rube Allyn. Now that you've caught it, how do you cook it? This book gives you a variety of recipes for each of 22 kinds of the fish you bring home. Also illustrated instructions for cleaning them. Size 5½x8½; 80 pages. Soft cover $1.50.

Coral Fishes by Tom Ravensdale. A guide to the saltwater aquarium. Every aspect of coral fish-keeping is here — a mine of information for the aquarist! Fifty color plates. Hard cover $7.95.

Marine Aquarium by R. F. O'Connell. All the latest information on this fascinating and fast-growing hobby. Sixty superb color photographs show the beauty of these intriguing fish. Practical advice on the salt-water aquarium and its fish. Revised edition. Soft cover $5.95, Hard cover $9.95.

Freshwater Aquarium by R. F. O'Connell. Complete and up-to-date guide for the fresh-water aquarium. The author explains in non-technical language how to set up and maintain an aquarium in peak condition. Fifty magnificent color illustrations. Hard cover $9.95.

If your dealer does not stock these books, mail your check to:

**GREAT OUTDOORS
PUBLISHING COMPANY**
4747 28th Street North
St. Petersburg, Fla., 33714

Florida residents include 4% sales tax
Code 1 - 15